PRAISE FOR *A MARRIAGE IN DOG YEARS*

"This funny, heartbreaking, spiritual book is a true love story, and once it has you in its grip it won't let you go. Nancy Balbirer's connection and devotion to her dog, Ira, her understanding of his role in her life— as a soul mate and a teacher—moved me deeply."

　—Tamar Geller, *New York Times* bestselling author of *The Loved Dog*

"Memoirs become memorable when the voice of the narrator reaches out to create a relationship you don't want to end. It took me all of about, say, eleven minutes to bond with the lovely, funny, and totally appealing Nancy Balbirer, author of the lovely, funny, and totally appealing *A Marriage in Dog Years*. If you have ever loved a dog or a person or had to say goodbye and somehow keep on going, this touching book will charm and move you. I enjoyed reading it very much."

　　　　　—George Hodgman, author of *Bettyville*

A

—

MARRIAGE *in*

DOG YEARS

ALSO BY NANCY BALBIRER

Take Your Shirt Off and Cry: A Memoir of Near-Fame Experiences

A

—

MARRIAGE *in*

DOG YEARS

—

a Memoir

NANCY BALBIRER

Published by Little A, New York

www.apub.com

Amazon, the Amazon logo, and Little A are trademarks of Amazon.com,
Inc., or its affiliates.

ISBN-13: 9781503940024 (hardcover)
ISBN-10: 1503940020 (hardcover)
ISBN-13: 9781503940017 (paperback)
ISBN-10: 1503940012 (paperback)

Cover design by Janet Perr

Printed in the United States of America

First edition

A

—

MARRIAGE *in*

DOG YEARS

AUTHOR'S NOTE

Some names and identifying details have been changed to protect the privacy of individuals.

For Boo Boo Bear

Prologue

I am driving in the middle lane on the 10 Freeway in Los Angeles, headed east, when my car, which has inexplicably begun to slow down, comes to a full stop. I press the pedal to the mat and fiddle with the ignition, but it's no use—the car is totally lifeless. *I am going to die,* I think, as I glance into my rearview mirror to watch the traffic careening toward me and then veering to the left or right before whizzing by. Fumbling for my almost-out-of-juice flip phone, I call my newish boyfriend, Sam, with whom I have just had lunch.

"My car's dead!" I shout. "And I'm on the freeway!"

"Can you get over to the side?" he shouts back.

"No—I'm stuck in the middle lane!"

"Where?"

"Just past Centinela—"

"Just past Centinela?"

"Yes!"

"But before Bundy?"

"Yes!"

"Hold on!" he yells. "Don't move . . . *I'll be right there . . .*"

Though I want to, I don't quite believe Sam will find me as I sit stranded on a busy Southern California freeway during peak hour. But even if he does, then what? How can I possibly escape unscathed? Nevertheless, there is nothing for me to do but wait and weep in abject terror, while everything that has led me to this moment on the freeway—plus an endless cavalcade of steel—flashes before my eyes.

I am an actress.

Like my car, I occasionally work.

In the past eighteen months, I've been hired and then fired from one of the biggest sitcoms of all time, hired and then mostly cut out of *another* of the biggest sitcoms of all time, and admonished by my *Valley of the Dolls*–ish agent for having too-small tits and something called "carb face."

I am, for the most part, miserable pursuing the only thing I ever loved or was even remotely good at. Even though I have never been more depressed or more lost in my life, I cannot—will not—quit trying to make it as an actress. Because even if it is a road more perilous to my psyche than the one on which I am currently braced, breaking up with my career of choice is out of the question: nothing petrifies me more than being a failure.

And speaking of failure, my car has done this before—on canyon hills, rain-drenched boulevards, movie-studio lots—always inopportune, embarrassing, dicey, but never death-defying. But like my career, I can't seem to quit my ride because, *unlike* my career, it is fabulous and I love it. Just a year ago, I'd been in an accident with a drunk driver who nearly killed me but instead totaled my previous car, leaving me with three broken ribs and a thematically shiteous end to what had been a total crash-and-burn year in Los Angeles. The insurance money was paltry but enough to buy a used 1991 midnight-blue Volkswagen Cabriolet convertible, with a stripy, limited-edition interior by the fashion designer Étienne Aigner, from a British girl in Manhattan Beach. It had "low spark" according to the mechanic who checked it out for me, but so did I lately. And for barely $1,000, I couldn't really afford to say no.

And just as I'm thinking about how harebrained this decision really was—as drivers slam on their horns and brakes, swerving to avoid splattering me and all those Étienne Aigner stripes across the asphalt—Sam calls me.

"I'm coming up," he yells. "On your left!"

"What do I do?" I cry, whipping around to see his Saab racing up behind me.

"Crack open the door!" he commands. "I'm slowing down and I'm gonna open the door. When I say 'jump,' open your door and jump in!"

"But—"

"Open your door! Now! *Nowwwww! Nowwwww!*"

Sam and his car have pulled up to my left; he leans over, flings open the passenger-side door.

"Jump!" he screams.

I dive in and slam the door shut, and Sam hits the gas. We zoom off, and though I am still shaking and traumatized, I am at the same time dazzled. Can it be that this nice guy who can pick a good restaurant is Superman, Batman, Iron Man, and Mighty Mouse all rolled into one? This slightly depressed Jewish intellectual is also a superhero?

Who knew?

But what I *did* know as we sped away that afternoon, leaving behind both my Cabriolet and my previous existence, was that though I had definitely been falling for this sweet, piano-playing law student, from that moment on, I was madly, incontrovertibly in love. I was the chick tied to the tracks, and he the dashing swashbuckler who would ultimately rescue me from far more than just extreme bodily harm.

I vowed to one day return the favor, to save Sam should he ever be down on his luck or in peril (though hopefully not on a freeway, since I also swore to never drive on one of those again). Leaping into his car and my new life, I was a damsel binding herself to her knight in shining Saab, ready to gamble on a future I couldn't possibly imagine.

I will amazingly forget about this moment, or not forget so much as push it to the far reaches of my mind, until one day when the memory will come to me in a flash and I will see us on that stretch of the 10, speeding off into the sunset, and it will occur to me that I had been so moved by the romance, the love, the chivalry of it all, that I had failed to notice we were not traveling west, but east—away from the sun.

JULY

One

LOVE SAVES THE DAY

There used to be this yoga class in Chelsea that met on Saturdays at noon called Love Saves the Day. Even though I was what you'd call a foul-weather yogi, only showing up to practice when I felt crappy about myself (as if sweaty twisting while hearing a Rumi poem would make me a better person), I still managed to make it there pretty much every week. The proceeds for the class benefited a different cause each month, which was perfect for a multitasking mom with little "me time": I could exercise my body *and* my existential angst while *also* trying to save the world.

One steamy Saturday, the day before Independence Day, class had just let out, and though I had to get home to walk my dog, Ira, I paused briefly on the street to talk to a friend. I knew I had to run—Ira's bladder had been working overtime, thus necessitating more and more frequent trips outside—but, in a post-practice haze of yogic good cheer, I lingered.

I don't remember what we were chatting about—the yoga, maybe, or the stiff air—but somehow, whatever it was segued into a conversation about my five-year-old daughter's Brazilian babysitter. With my daughter starting kindergarten in a couple of months, we would no longer be needing her services; I thought my friend, with three children of her own, might be interested in hiring her.

"Is she young?" my friend inquired.

"She is," I said, "but totally experienced—*and* a trained nurse, which has been a major bonus."

"Is she hot?" my friend asked.

"Uh, she is, yes," I said. "Why?"

My friend laughed and shook her head.

"You employed a *young, hot, Brazilian* babysitter? Are you interested in staying married?"

Now it was my turn to laugh. Had some bizarre combo of the heat and savasana propelled us through the space-time continuum and into the middle of an *I Love Lucy* episode? Maybe this was the deal for my friend and her banker hubby—what with his "business trips" and "work dinners" and off-hours spent with eyes glued to the wireless device he always had Velcroed to his paw—and she had to be super vigilant lest he "stray." But an Eisenhower-era dynamic wasn't remotely the one Sam and I shared, nor was he the type to cheat, nor, quite frankly, was it my concern. But, if I could easily scoff at the innuendo, something about the question itself I found harder to dismiss:

Are you interested in staying married?

The answer was *yes—yes, of course.* And yet, while I stood listening to my friend expound on the various celebrities whose husbands had *shtupped* the nanny, the question continued to loom, demanding my attention, like some sort of Zen koan meant to enlighten by provoking what the monks call the "Great Doubt."

Sam and I were having problems, and though I didn't realize it at the time, I was making believe that we weren't. Suddenly, my friend's facetious little query had me falling through a booby trap of other disquieting moments, like one that had occurred several months prior: someone had described me as a "happily married woman," whereupon I blurted out, "Married, yes; happily . . . no."

Shaken though I was by my reply, I didn't spend too much time thinking about it. Instead, I chose to view the whole thing as a slip made late at night after one too many glasses of Pinot Grigio, never allowing the question *Are you interested in staying married?* to creep into my mind.

And that was weird—it wasn't as if I'd never asked myself the question before.

I'd asked it, for instance, when I was four months pregnant and Sam walked out of his job at a law firm and then fled to the hills of Western Massachusetts to attend a weeklong "silence retreat." And when I was in the waiting room of my ob-gyn's office, noticing I was the only preggo sitting there alone, sans baby daddy. I'd asked it when he told me he wanted to open a wine bar / restaurant in which we'd have to invest all our savings. And I'd most certainly asked it when out of the blue I began obsessively daydreaming about having sex with a guy I'd known in college. But, in the aftermath of the recent gaffe, I hadn't asked myself whether I was interested in staying married. I'd just treated the episode like an aching tooth you pray doesn't turn out to need a root canal: I'd ignored it and hoped for the best.

There are times, though, when the questions you don't ask yourself manage to find you anyway. I may not have been willing to admit, yet, how bad things really were, but the truth was about to come barreling to the surface. Because, like a troubled tooth, when a marriage is in crisis, there's only so long you can pretend before dull pain turns into searing agony.

Sam and I at that moment in time had been married for eleven years and together for thirteen. One evening not long after the miraculous freeway rescue mission, in the merry month of May, beneath a crystalline California sky, we were married on the first day of a new moon. This, according to our rabbi, was especially auspicious: new moons—those barely visible curved slips in the sky—not only signify new beginnings but attest to "the unequivocal faith one must have to venture forth in darkness." It was our most favorite thing about our wedding date, one to which we would repeatedly return—our "moon mantra," we called it. *We do not need light,* we'd say. *As long as we are together, we will find our way, we will never be lost.* And, for a long time, it was true.

Then, after four years of marriage, we were confronted with infertility. We stepped aboard the IVF Habitrail, and though it was only six months from diagnosis to conception, Sam and I, during the process and throughout the subsequent pregnancy, became increasingly isolated from each other. Wounds appearing out of nowhere were harbored; resentments were clung to like plastic rafts in a tsunami. Even after the arrival, one midwinter day, of the perfect baby girl we nicknamed "the Bear," after Boo Boo Bear, we quarreled so often and so bitterly that it seemed as though the darkness had won and we just couldn't find our way out. *Is it over? Oh my god, is it over?* Round and round I'd spin, searching Sam's eyes to see if I could glean how he felt or what he thought, yet unable to actually say these words out loud, so terrified was I to know his response. Even to hear him say the word *over* in an entirely different context could send me into paroxysms of panic. I began to feel as though we were locked in a bad dream, the kind where you have enough consciousness to know that forces beyond your control are preventing you from getting somewhere, being with someone, making contact.

We went to couples counseling and "worked on it." Things got better. Or . . . better*ish*, let's say, and there was a sense that we'd come to some version of our new normal, all the while growing into parents more besotted with our beautiful Bear each passing day.

I wasn't quite sure what to make of the persistent unease, the lingering sort of ennui that characterized our day-to-day in the five years since the Bear had arrived—what was at the root of it or how, exactly, it had come to pass. We settled into an arrangement of mutual avoidance, a dual complicity by which we silently agreed to pretend that the conflicts we continually swept under the rug weren't causing a lump to grow in the center of our living room. We began to spend more and more time apart, and when we did hang out we never really talked the way we once had so much as made conversation, like coworkers on a menial job, willing the hours to pass. If, in fact, the genesis of our issues was the fertility crisis, why, then, I wondered to myself, since we'd made it through the shit-show and to the other side, had things never gone back to the way they were? Or was it that we were now parents, which added another layer to our dynamic that made reverting to any sort of "before" impossible anyway? Was this just marriage? Was this just how everyone was? I didn't know. Just as I didn't know then, standing on that street corner, sweaty and gross, making small talk in the towering inferno that is a New York City summer, that I was about to spend the next year trying to figure it out.

The only thing I knew for sure as I bade my friend goodbye and fled toward home was that the mere mention of my marriage, even in glib terms, poked at me as I hurried away, like the niggling tag in my yoga pants I needed to snip but always forgot about until halfway through the first downward-facing dog.

~

Arriving home, I found myself facing a different kind of dog than the one I'd left two hours before, one that was now sluggish and shivering, sitting next to a pool of piss.

"Ira," I said. "What is it, sweetheart?"

Tail thwacking the floor, Ira slunk furtively into my embrace, his head hung in shame. Like most beagles, Ira's eyes always betrayed a hint of melancholy, but as I gently lifted his chin and gazed into those chocolate-brown hound eyes, they appeared not just sad, but confused and afraid. I pulled out my phone and called Ira's longtime vet, Jim;

because it was the day before a holiday, the office was closing early, but he told me if I hurried over, he would see him.

Fifteen minutes later, we were at Chelsea Animal Hospital, and as I described Ira's symptoms, Jim performed a manual exam. "He's lost a lot of weight and he's pretty dehydrated," Jim said, pinching Ira's fur between his fingers. "When did you first start noticing a change?"

"I feel like this just happened. Like, all of a sudden, you know?"

Jim nodded, soberly, as he took Ira's temperature.

"I mean, the only thing is that he's been peeing a lot lately."

Jim nodded again. "Well, let's run some tests, see if we can figure out what's up."

Jim called for some assistance; blood was drawn, X-rays taken, and then we waited. Ira, still on the examination table, clung to me as he always did when we were at the vet: front legs wrapped around my shoulders, paws gripping my neck. And as I stood soothing him, staring at a framed Stephen Huneck print entitled *My Dog's Brain*, which illustrated crucial canine thoughts like "sniffing dog butts" and "food," in *my* brain the question played on repeat mode:

When did you first start noticing a change?

I flipped through my mental file cabinet, trying to recall even the tiniest sign. There was the peeing . . . and he had randomly thrown up the week before . . . or was it the week before that? Ira began to pant, and his grip around my neck became more intense.

"OK, OK, relax, doggy," I said, hugging him and massaging him behind his ears. "It's gonna be OK . . ."

Just then, the door swung open and Jim walked in, and somehow, before he said anything, I knew it wasn't OK.

I hear "It's his kidneys," but the words come out of sync with Jim's mouth, like in the bad Japanese monster movies I watched as a child.

These words are followed by other words, like "renal failure . . . it's not good . . . he can't recover . . . terminal."

I remember feeling dizzy, rootless, and the sensation of hot and cold simultaneously whirling in my head, like I had stood up too quickly. I went through a panicked attempt to fathom the unfathomable; my thoughts soared like darts trying to make contact with a moving target: *How is this happening? I took immaculate care of him, feeding him only the highest-quality organic, raw, absurdly expensive dog food, the ingredients of which had been gleaned with scientific precision by a team of researchers who had unearthed what wolves would have once upon a time eaten in the wild, whereupon every last grass-fed, additive-free item was then carefully sourced and culled with the use of modern technology, so that each bite would make my beloved pet feel as though he were living out his life in the pages of a Jack London novel. Ira's innards, what with all of these premium-grade, wholesome ingredients, should have been as pristine as Gwyneth Paltrow's—not coursing with an ever-increasing toxicity that was silently killing him. HOW, HOW COULD IT BE . . . ? Oh my god, oh my god, my dog . . . oh my god, please, god, please . . . no.*

Simultaneously, I began grasping at other straws, pleading with my well-meaning vet for answers:

"But isn't there something . . . ? Isn't there some sort of treatment?"

Jim sighed, shaking his head. "I mean, look, we can give him fluids, try to get him hydrated. We could treat the symptoms, but it'll be, you know, palliative."

Palliative.

"I honestly don't know, with these numbers, if he'll make it through the weekend."

We were both stroking Ira, who was standing on the table between us, panting.

"Are you saying I need to . . . ?" I began to cry.

"I mean," he said gently, "people do. Some people would."

I was lost, sobbing.

"You don't have to do that this minute, I'm just . . . look, we could see how he does with some subcutaneous fluids and some antinausea meds and some vitamins to, you know, give him energy."

"With that stuff," I choked out, "what would that do? What would it give us?"

"Time. Maybe some time."

"At best, what kind of time?"

"Maybe, I dunno . . . three weeks?"

I nodded, wiping tears. "Is he in any pain?"

"No. He's just sick."

Ira, standing up on his hind legs, front legs wrapping once again around my neck, began to lick my face, my tears, the stream of snot running from my nose, as though it were ambrosia.

I pulled back slightly, looking into his eyes. It was all so inconceivable. This did not look like a soul ready to leave this world; the only thing he looked ready for was dinner. I knew I couldn't let go—not yet. It was all too much, too soon. And if he wasn't in pain and I had no indication from him that he was, then time, and the buying of it, was good enough for me.

I called Sam briefly and told him the news. "Come home," he said. "Just come home and we'll deal with it . . ."

Jim reminded me that they would be closed until Tuesday and that if anything happened or he got worse in the next two days, to take him into the twenty-four-hour emergency vet near Fifth Avenue. He called the front desk to assemble fluid bags, needles, vitamins, and meds; he gave me his cell phone number and a long, compassionate hug, during which my tears began to flow once again.

"How did this happen?" I asked finally. "What caused it?"

"No one knows, really," he said.

"So—there was nothing I could have done to prevent this? I mean, did I . . . not take him out enough and inadvertently put too much strain on his kidneys from not, you know, walking him enough so that—"

"No, no—nothing like that," he insisted. "It's just . . ." He sighed. "It's just bad luck is all. With kidney failure, it's just a case of really bad luck."

Bad luck, I thought, *kidney failure.* It was not lost on me that my dog—one of the most unabashedly glamorous, sassy, truly magnificent-looking creatures I have ever known—was suffering from what killed Jean Harlow. And like the tragic Harlow, who'd died at the age of twenty-six, Ira, blessed with youth and beauty, was being felled by a simple case of bad luck. No cause and no cure; impossible though it all seemed, we were now on borrowed time.

~

Someone once described being diagnosed with a terminal illness as receiving a threatening letter from someone that you don't even know. And Ira's, it seemed, arrived with no return address. Worse, he appeared to be taking his "letter" to heart, as if he'd read it and, heeding its warning, was surrendering without further ado. From the moment we arrived home, his condition worsened, steadily declining throughout the evening. He wouldn't eat; he just sat in front of his food bowl, staring at its contents while I stood next to him, cooking dinner, wondering what to do next.

"Whatsa matter with Ira, Mama?" I turned to see the Bear peeking in the kitchen doorway. She was wearing a costume nurse's cap and holding a plastic stethoscope.

"He's sick, sweetie," I said.

"Does he have a boo-boo?"

"No, he's just sick, sweetie. He's very sick."

The Bear sat down, donned her stethoscope, and held it to Ira's chest.

"Is he gonna get a shot?"

"I'm not sure yet. We have to see."

The Bear decided that Ira needed to be read a story. She couldn't actually read but faked it superbly, and she ran to her bedroom to fetch one of the less heinous versions of *Sleeping Beauty*.

Following dinner, Sam and I administered Ira's meds and fluids, after which he limped off, retreating to the confines of our bedroom closet. I wanted to take him over to the emergency vet right then, but our current financial situation was such that Sam insisted we give it some time before incurring the cost of hospitalization.

Throughout the night, Ira remained in the closet. He was restless and his sleep, if it came, fitful. This in turn made me incredibly anxious. I was petrified that his behavior was indicative of his imminent demise. I thus found myself waking up just about every hour to check on him, believing that the act of rousing myself would will away the Angel of Death. Finally, at about three in the morning, I gave up on sleep and joined Ira in the closet.

Sitting on the floor in the pitch black, knees drawn into my chest, I am like Jonah, swallowed up inside the whale, an opportunist, praying for deliverance from a god I mostly ignored. As if in a sort of meditative trance, I am hyperpresent yet, at the same time, find myself suddenly swimming in the pool of our past. I see Sam and myself, two months after our wedding, at the Beverly Center mall in Los Angeles, looking at an adorable beagle puppy asleep in a cage, then asking to check him out. Even before we are ensconced in the play area, we are sold; he is ours. We free-associate names:

Beagles are English, right? Let's name him George.

Oh, that's good—after George Gershwin.

Oh, but wait—George Gershwin died young.

True, true . . .

But his brother Ira lived to be something like eighty-six—

Ira . . . I love it! . . .

I love it, too . . . it's perfection!

Ira . . .

Ira . . .

Ira. Our first baby. Our wedding gift to each other, at a time when our partnership was the perfect alignment of taste, sensibility, humor, and love. So much that transpired was shaped by that day and the fateful whim to take home that puppy: how closely entwined, how integral he would become to our story. How we delighted over his unswerving devotion to pizza crusts, his enthusiasm for the random dead palm kernels found on Los Angeles side streets, his relish for rolling in the brown grass of Laurel Canyon dog park and lazy hikes up Runyon Canyon. How hard it made us laugh that, no matter how many picturesque West Village streets we took him down, he would never take a dump until he sniffed his way to the tree in front of Sarah Jessica Parker's town house—a feat so uncanny we began to refer to him as "Sarah Jessica Poo-Poo."

As I lift Ira gingerly onto my lap, my mind floods with silent movie-memories, and I begin to see our marriage refracted in dog years: Ira is one, we buy a house; Ira is three, we sell the house; Ira is four, Sam and I take a second honeymoon; Ira is five, the Bear is born; Ira is six, Sam and I open a wine bar; Ira is ten, I publish a book. Moments zoom by like shooting stars: Ira running around in circles, howling when we dance, trembling when we fight, lying between us in bed as we sleep. His role in our saga morphing from catalyst to supporting player to voiceless voice of reason to, so often for me, substitute partner.

When I was worn to a frazzle during the dark days of infertility and complicated pregnancy, there were times when I was so down, so depressed, I could barely get out of bed. And in those days, it was Ira who became my link to the outside world. How often I would bemoan the chore of pulling my ass out of my cozy vat of self-pity to take him out so that he could relieve himself, take some air, get some exercise. He would skip down the street on his retractable leash, nose to the ground, pendulous beagle ears swinging, tail held high, wagging gaily, with me trailing forlornly behind. Every now and then, he would turn to glance back at me, tongue out and face lit up in that silly, slightly demented smile. Beckoning me to follow, as if to say, *It is all so fun and exciting to sniff out our next story; there's* always *a new story—come with me! Come with me!*

And I would soon come to understand that I wasn't walking him at all; he was walking me.

I don't know how long I was sitting there before Sam opened the closet door.

"What are you doing?" he whispered.

"I'm taking the dog to the emergency room," I said.

Sam knelt down, putting his hand on Ira's head.

"Maybe we should just let nature take its course."

I didn't want a fight, but I was resolute.

"I don't care what it costs—I'll sell my jewelry, sell my clothes, anything. But I can't let him suffer like this."

Sam nodded. "You want me to come with you?"

"No. Stay with the Bear. It's OK. I'll go alone."

I gathered up Ira in a blanket, and in the predawn darkness, I dove into a taxi and headed toward Fifth Avenue.

~

After staying in intensive care for two days, Ira returned to Jim and Chelsea Animal Hospital for another two days. Several thousand dollars later, his condition was stabilized and he was ready to be released.

"How long do you think we have?" I asked Jim. "I mean . . . realistically."

"To be honest," he said, "I wouldn't be surprised if I see you back here tomorrow or Saturday. Maybe you have till the end of the weekend—at best a couple of weeks. Depends on how he responds to treatment. But we're not talking about a year or something."

I nodded. At least I wasn't stunned anymore. Jim put his hand on my shoulder; he was in "manage expectations mode," clearly the suckiest part of his job.

"I'm sorry," he said. "He's really sick."

I nodded again. "Do you think we need to . . . you know . . . ?"

"No—I don't. Not yet. Let's see how he does. He's stabilized; he's alert, wagging his tail . . ."

"How will I know? How will I know when . . . if . . . I need to let him go?"

Jim sighed. "I think you'll know. I mean, he's not eating yet. If you can't get him to eat when you get him home, or over the next day or so, then you'll know."

There was a haze over Chelsea as we wended our way home that made even the heat seem gray. Jagged beams of sunlight glinted off shop windows and cars, and as I cradled Ira in my arms, passing people would look at us and smile. "Aww—how cute!" they'd say, as if this were just a normal day and I were carrying my dog because he was adorable and it was all good.

We're not talking about a year, he had said.

But Jim would be wrong. Ira *would* last a year; in fact, he would, miraculously, last for a year and twenty-one days from when his condition was first diagnosed as terminal.

He would not eat any food that sweltering summer day after Jim released him for what we thought was his final journey home. But sometime late in the afternoon of the following day, Ira would be sitting beside Sam and me on the couch, both of us petting him, both of us so certain the end was near. The Bear would be watching *The King and I*, and halfway through the number "Shall We Dance?," as the music swelled and the dance reached its full exuberance, Ira would eat a meatball from Whole Foods out of my hand. Sam would look at me, smile, his green eyes made even greener by the tears beginning to form, and say, "Well, I guess it's not over, then, is it?" And for the first time in forever, he would take my hand and pull me in for a long hug. It would be remarkable to me how delicious, in spite of everything, his hug still felt—just like the very first time, as we stood on a Los Angeles street, his embrace felt like home. *No,* I would say silently, breathing his being into mine, *it's not over, nor will I let it be.*

In sickness and in health, till death do us part. Faith in the dark.

The words would resound in my head as I made a silent pact with myself: *I will not let anything go; I will not let anything die; I will save everything and everyone who needs saving.* And, for the next year and twenty-one days, I would believe with every piece of my being that fulfilling these promises was within my power, that love, even if it was palliative, could indeed save the day.

Two

My Doggy, My Self

I once read about a Japanese scientist who found empirical evidence that people and their dogs tend to look alike. According to his conclusions, it all boils down to this: people are drawn to (and ultimately choose) dogs that resemble themselves. The psychological explanation for such a phenomenon (aside from garden-variety narcissism) is something called "mere-exposure effect," which is basically a fancy way of saying that people tend to like things that are familiar.

Looking back, I can't say that I was struck by the "familiar" when I first laid eyes on Ira. For reasons I can't explain, one morning a few months after Sam and I got back from our honeymoon, I found myself taking the escalator to the sixth floor of the Beverly Center and wandering into the pet store. Where I was actually going that day, and for what purpose, was quickly forgotten. Instead, I stood mesmerized for forty-five minutes, observing a beagle puppy roughhousing a Jack Russell puppy in a display cage. The Jack Russell would gamely wrestle with the beagle for a bit, then, having had enough, would turn to stumble away. The beagle would allow the Jack Russell to take maybe a few paces, then, diving through the air Hulk Hogan–style, he'd attack him from behind.

I was spellbound.

The particulars, Sharpied on a note card on the side of the cage, said the following: MALE, BEAGLE, DOB: 7/27/99.

Huh, I thought to myself. *A Leo. I always liked Leos.*

A few days later, I dragged Sam into the pet store. Within moments, he, also smitten, slapped a wire crate and the male beagle Leo onto his Visa card.

Looks-wise? I don't know.

Once, at a dog birthday party, we won a contest for "Owner and Dog Who Most Resemble Each Other." But, aside from us both having reddish hair, I honestly never saw it.

What I did recognize in Ira was an emotional affinity, a kindred soul with whom I felt an almost immediate connection and devotion. Within days of taking him home from the pet store, I began to notice him gazing at me in a peculiar way—and not just in a typical "fur baby" looking adoringly at his "mother" way, but with an uncanny mix of empathy and identification as if we were somehow of the same tribe.

One early morning, I woke up to find him with his head on my pillow, just looking at me. How long he had been lying there observing me I hadn't a clue, but I didn't move a muscle. Instead, I just lay still, peering back at him. After several minutes, I was overtaken by a wave of not just love but visceral identification I can only describe as the kind one experiences in early-stage soul-mate moments. I know it sounds bonkers (even for California), but here's the thing: in a very short amount of time, I felt loved by Ira—*truly loved* for all that I was (and wasn't)—in a way I hadn't felt loved before, and not just by another animal but even by family, friends, and some of my most intimate romantic partners. At times, I even thought Ira loved me more than Sam did.

I wondered, then, if it was possible that we as dog owners might make our selections not because we see ourselves in the *faces* of our potential pooches but because we intuit that their interior lives may in fact align with our own. I knew it was likely that we endowed dogs with our interests or with the things we loved so that we felt validated about those choices, but did we maybe also use them as mirrors in order to discover ourselves more fully?

Ira was not the first pet-store dog who had captivated me. In my early pre-Sam days in Los Angeles, I had a habit of making special trips to the mall for no reason other than to hold puppies. I didn't know anything then about pet stores and puppy mills and their atrocities (in fact, I wouldn't learn about any of that until many years after we brought Ira home), but one day, after buying underwear at Bloomingdale's, I passed by a window where I saw a cairn terrier puppy staring out. I stopped and stared back. The puppy, plopped atop shredded newspaper and with nothing else in the cage but a half-empty water bottle, looked bummed and lonely.

"Me, too, honey," I whispered, pressing my forehead against the glass. "Me, too."

I went in and expressed interest in the puppy to one of the many disaffected pet-store staffers. Within seconds, it was sprung from its window-cage, and the two of us were whisked into a private area for "bonding time." Though my intent was to offer solace to this tiny, motherless creature, the minute the cuddling began, it became obvious that the puppy wasn't the only one in need of consoling. I began sharing my sob story about being a displaced New Yorker and how much I missed things like bagels, and how the bagels in LA were really more like bread blocks with holes, except for the bagels I'd had when I did a guest appearance on *Seinfeld*, but that was only because Jerry had the bagels flown in overnight from New York, and the minute I found *that* out, I couldn't stop eating them, to the point where I ate so many of those goddamn bagels the people in wardrobe told me I needed a girdle, which was both humiliating *and* confusing because I didn't know they even made girdles anymore.

Something about this exercise buoyed me so much that, even though I knew I couldn't have a dog at that point in my life, I went back the next week and the next and the next for more cuddles and one-sided convo. By my second visit, I felt the puppy, who was a girl, needed a name. For my entire life, I'd been completely obsessed with movies—especially old ones—so I decided to name her after one of my favorite fictive movie actresses. I thought about *Margo*, after Bette Davis's Margo Channing, or *Neely*, after Patty Duke's Neely O'Hara, but she didn't really look like a *Margo* or a *Neely*. I settled on *Anna*, after the aging, out-of-work, impossibly chic Czech actress who lives in a dump, played by Sally Kirkland in the title role. Each visit, we'd hole up in the little play area, and I'd lift Anna's furry little face to my nose so I could smell her delicious puppy breath and tell her all about how shitty this or that audition went while she licked my cheek and tried to eat my hair. It killed me that I had to leave her there, but because it was a case of the right dog at the wrong time, somehow I'd tear myself away. Then, one day, I showed up and little Anna was gone. She'd been bought a few days before, and though I was glad she finally had a forever home, I was heartbroken and never returned to the pet store until the fateful day when I wandered in and saw Ira kicking the shit out of the Jack Russell.

Later, when I brought Sam in and we played with Ira in that same play area, my heart bubbled over with memories of Anna and of how badly I had wanted her. I had thought I would never find love *or* be able to take home one of those adorable puppies. *All my dreams are coming true,* I remember thinking as I watched Sam play with Ira. *Who is luckier than me?*

~

Only a few weeks after the renal-failure diagnosis, Ira was on the mend and more at peace than I had seen him in ages. The antinausea meds Jim had prescribed seemed to make a difference; the various vitamins we hid in his food did, too. But it was the subcutaneous fluids we administered to "balance electrolytes and replenish hydration" that seemed to be the game changer. Even while having to lie still twice a day for a full ten minutes with a large needle poking out of the fur between his shoulder blades to receive the fluids, Ira was bright-eyed, waggy-tailed, and full of good cheer.

"He seems so happy, so relieved," I was telling Sam as we shared fluid duty early one morning. "It's as though he recognizes that life is a gift, and now that he's stabilized and feeling better, he wants to lead each day as a thank-you note . . ."

Sam looked up to monitor the fluid bag's level, then, looking at me, he smiled.

"What?" I asked.

"Nothing."

"I think he gets it—I really do . . ."

Sam nodded.

"You think I'm projecting?"

Sam paused, shrugged, and smiled again. I smiled back.

Ever since our embrace on the couch that fateful day when Ira ate his Whole Foods meatball, there had been between us lingering feelings of affection and warmth, flowing as easily as the saline through Ira's hydrating tube.

"Maybe," Sam said, finally, "a little . . ."

"You don't think he has his own feelings about it? His own will to live?"

"I think," Sam said slowly, "he definitely knows how much it means to you that he recovers."

"Well, of course I'm happy . . . and relieved, too."

Sam nodded.

I nodded back. "I mean, aren't you?" I asked.

"Aren't I what?"

"Happy?"

"Yes."

"And relieved . . . ?"

"Of course."

There was a pause. For some reason, I had this deep need for Sam and me to be on the same page when it came to Ira and to be equally invested in his recovery—as if Sam's stake in our dog's health said something about his interest in me or, more importantly, us. Ira's situation had already given us a renewed appreciation for each another, and I couldn't help but feel that if he survived for any length of time, we'd be closer for having gone through the stress of his illness together. Likewise, if—god forbid—he died, we'd be together in our grief. I felt strange and guilty positing about Ira's survival in this way, but he was our dog and our glue. If there was anything aside from our child that signified our coupledom, it was him.

"Look," Sam said, "I just don't want us to get our hopes up. He's OK for the moment, but I think we need to be realistic."

I nodded again.

Reflexively, I began to gather Ira's big, floppy hound ears into my hands, pretending to tie them into a bow on the top of his head. They were never quite long enough to become a bow, and yet I did this at least once a day, always surprised to see that his ears came up short, before abandoning my pursuit altogether. Sam took my hand as I struggled to make sense of the non-bow.

"Hey," he said.

I stopped and looked at him.

"I *am* happy." Sam squeezed my hand. "And relieved."

"OK," I said, squeezing back.

"I mean, I don't know that I want to 'lead each day as a thank-you note,' but . . ."

This made us both laugh, after which we stopped and looked at each other, holding the gaze for several seconds. *How long*, I wondered, *has it been since we did something like that? Since we actually took the time to look at each other on purpose and not accidentally?* I couldn't remember. Instead, I remembered other things about him and me and us as we knelt on the floor of our tiny kitchen, our dog and his tubes between us. Scenes of other times I may or may not have projected my feelings, dreams, and worldview onto my dog soared through my mind, erupting like fireworks, before twinkling and fading into oblivion. I found myself still convinced that, while his tastes and mine were very much in tune, Ira was his own dog with his own proclivities.

Take, for example, his passion for Dolly Parton: certainly it's true that I *also* admire Dolly Parton, but it was not until Ira entered my world that I began to spend entire afternoons listening repeatedly to the album *Jolene* or the soundtrack to *The Best Little Whorehouse in Texas*.

The Dolly discovery was made one afternoon in Los Angeles when he was a puppy of six, maybe seven, months old. Ira was sleeping soundly on the passenger seat of my car, and Dolly Parton's version of the song "Hard Candy Christmas" from the movie *The Best Little Whorehouse in Texas* came on.

Ira popped up, instantly awake, instantly alert. His nose began twitching, and his head began to bob up and down as if he were trying to catch a scent. Then he began to whimper. And he kept on whimpering until it got so intense that I pulled over to see whether he'd somehow been injured. Eventually, he stopped, and we drove on. Several days later, the same thing happened: we were in the car, Dolly came on singing "Hard Candy" from *Whorehouse*, and Ira, once again, rose from slumber, began to twitch, nose-bob, and cry. I shut off the music, and Ira was fine. I drove for a bit, turned on the tape, and . . . same thing. I turned off the music, and he quieted.

Maybe it's music, I thought to myself. *Maybe his giant hound ears get overwhelmed by music.*

Or was it . . . *Dolly?*

I fast-forwarded the tape. It landed in the middle of Ben Vereen singing "Magic to Do" from *Pippin*. I looked intently at Ira and . . . nothing. If anything, he seemed bored.

When I got home, I told Sam.

"I think Ira has a thing for Dolly Parton."

"What?"

"He's a fan."

Sam was nonplussed.

"Well," I said, qualifying, "let's not go overboard. He's *at least* a fan of her singing 'Hard Candy Christmas' from the movie version of *Best Little Whorehouse in Texas*—"

"Because that makes more sense than . . . his being 'a fan' of Dolly Parton's entire oeuvre?"

"Go ahead and make fun," I said, popping the tape of Dolly singing 'Hard Candy' into our stereo. "But this is some out-there shit . . ."

Sure enough, Ira began to twitch, nose-bob, and cry. And though Sam had to acknowledge there was clearly a real reaction, he insisted that our dog's response to Dolly either was a fluke or was generated by his sensing that it was I, his wacky owner, who had a hard-on for "Hard Candy Christmas."

"You're the one who loves Dolly Parton!" Sam insisted as we sat listening, our dog rolling on the floor at our feet. "And this is not just some random song—it's a song you *love* . . ."

It was true. I *do* really love her rendition of that song. And I also think Dolly Parton is terrific in general (who doesn't?). But so what? My love for Joni Mitchell knows no bounds, but I played *Blue* and *Ladies of the Canyon* in the car all the time, and whenever I did, Ira sat through them stone-faced. Barbra Streisand, Judy Garland, Edith Piaf, Kate Bush—I played them all ad nauseam in my house and in my car, and nary a peep out of my dog. No, Ira's impassioned response to Dolly was way more than just delusion on my part, though I wished I had more than just the *Whorehouse* soundtrack upon which to build a hypothesis.

Then, one sweltering afternoon several months later, I came across a tattered copy of the LP *Jolene* at a tag sale in Tarzana. I happily paid the twenty-five-cent list price and rushed away, eager to see its effect, if any, on my puppy. Well, all I can say is that Pavlov and his dog had nothing on my little beagle and me. From the moment the record began to spin on the turntable, Ira was on his back, snout in the air, rolling back and forth, snapping and snorting at imaginary antagonists, while I sat on the couch, watching him, utterly dumbfounded. Side two of *Jolene* begins with the plaintive yet soaring "I Will Always Love You," which most people attribute to Whitney Houston, but which is nevertheless a song written (and first performed) by Dolly Parton. Initially, Ira had little to no response, but as soon as Dolly got to the *Ah-eee-ah, will all-ways love youuuuu, ooh-ah-ah* part, he began, once again, to twitch, nose-bob, and whimper. For years, I had thought that the most bizarre thing I had ever seen as far as animals were concerned was a corgi who howled inconsolably anytime she heard Debussy's "Prélude à l'après-midi d'un faune." As batty as that was, Ira's Dolly thing was even more so, and I spent a lot of time coming up with crackpot theories.

I remembered reading a Roald Dahl story in his racy adult prose collection in which a stray cat is the reincarnation of the Hungarian composer Franz Liszt. The cat seems to appreciate pieces by Brahms, is decidedly *meh* on pieces by Schumann, and *adores* pieces by Liszt, the discovery of which brings about the past-life revelation. Since Dolly Parton was alive, I began to wonder whether perhaps Ira was the reincarnation of, say, Hank Williams, or some other country-music singer with crossover appeal—a dead member of the Carter family, for instance. Ira's "papers" claimed he was from a part of southeastern Kansas that bordered Missouri, and Missouri bordered Tennessee (home of Dolly Parton), which was certainly, at the very least, geographically thematic.

And the more we bonded, Ira and I, the more I found myself doing this thing where I would daydream about what he'd be like if he were human. Mostly, I fantasized that he'd be this extremely handsome redneck—good-natured, affectionate, romantic. I imagined him as the sort of guy who lit up any room into which he happened to saunter, a guy whose big, beautiful smile was as much his trademark as was his sweetness, one who enjoyed sassy and sophisticated big-city girls with whom he could enjoy living a life high on the hog. I figured that such a fellow—what with his humble roots and down-home charm—would have the sort of easygoing masculinity that could pull off a penchant for Dolly Parton in much the same way that a smoldering, urban Al Pacino type could carry off a predilection for opera.

I did not see, as I entertained friends or strangers with these anecdotes, how much it meant to me that people viewed my dog as wonderful and unique. I did not understand that my need to ascribe human foibles to Ira was about my own desire to connect. In fact, it wasn't until Ira won a free session with a renowned animal psychic in his doggy day care's Christmas grab bag that I began to grasp the level at which I was emotionally invested in any of this being real.

The psychic (who looked like a dark-haired, butch Renée Zellweger) flew in from Colorado, and we met for our appointment at Ira's doggy day care in West Hollywood. Amy, the day care owner, graciously let us use her office while she sat behind her desk, paying bills. The session consisted of Ira "talking" to me through the psychic in more or less a monologue about his life, thoughts, and feelings. He spoke of being put in a box and shipped away from the farm where he was born, then languishing at the mall until Sam and I took him home.

"You thought I was beautiful," he said via the gruff-voiced psychic, "and you were right—I am."

The boastfulness made me laugh.

"It's true," I said to the psychic. "He really is beautiful."

"It would be better if you talk directly to him," she instructed. "He's listening . . ."

I glanced over at Amy, who looked at me briefly, shrugged, and then went back to her busywork. After a few moments of silence, I spoke, as the psychic had commanded, directly to Ira.

"I'm glad you know you're beautiful, sweetheart," I told him, "because . . . well, it's true—you are."

"He is saying, 'Yes, I am, and so are you,'" the psychic Cyrano croaked. "He says, 'But you don't seem to think too much of yourself.'"

"I—I don't?"

"He says, 'No, Mommy, you don't. But I wish you did.'"

For the next forty-five minutes, I listened to all manner of candid, deeply astute observations as to my nature: how I moved through life with way too much "trepidation" (his word), how I lacked foresight and aggressiveness with respect to my acting career. Ira "told me" that I drank too much wine (I did), that I worried too much about what people thought of me all the time (I did), and that I didn't consider my ambitions worthy enough (I didn't). He "wondered aloud" if I might consider overhauling the palette of my home to include more "animal prints and vibrant colors, like red," as they might give me "energy." Finally, Ira told me that he was "proud every day" to have me as his mother and that, in case I didn't know or was somehow unaware, our black cat was "a giant asshole."

I suppose I wasn't surprised that my low self-esteem figured in or was something bandied about, since it would be remarkably easy to guess under the circumstances (um, hello, I was spending the better part of an afternoon with a dog psychic), *but* how a stranger could know about our assholic Burmese cat or my penchant for wine and neutral colors was beyond me.

"You heard all that, right?" I asked Amy once the psychic had packed up her psychic bag, put on her psychic coat, and split for the private sessions she had scheduled at the beach. "I mean . . . that was crazy, right?"

"It was definitely crazy. But fun and, hey, free, you know?"

I sat down in the chair in front of Amy's desk, and Ira jumped into my lap and began to lick my face.

"Do you think it's true," I continued, "that she 'communicated' with him and he, like, told her this shit?"

"I think there's something to it, I really do," Amy said, leaning back in her chair and propping her feet up on her desk. "How totally accurate it is, how exact the stuff is she claims they're saying to us, I mean . . . I dunno. But, Nance—the most important thing you heard today you kinda already knew, right?"

"You mean about my drinking too much wine?"

"No!" Amy laughed. "About how much he loves you. In the end, isn't that all that matters?"

It certainly was. And suffice it to say that when we drove off that day in my little convertible, Ira on my lap, Dolly on my tape deck, I was not only moved by the many insights imparted, I honestly felt closer to and more cheered by my dog than anyone I had ever known.

When we got home that day and I told Sam the story of the psychic, he wasn't buying it. He poked so many holes in her psychic spiel, he made it hard to dispute that I had been had.

"The cat isn't even *black*," Sam said matter-of-factly. "He's dark brown."

Be that as it may, I wasn't the only one in our marriage given to a soupçon of anthropomorphizing: the second it became clear that our Ira was one of the most popular, beloved dogs at his doggy day care, Sam, the party-pooping realist who only ever laughed at my musings, my experiences, my what have you, began singing a *very* different tune. Perhaps it was a result of Sam's having grown up a disaffected youth in 1980s Los Angeles, surrounded by the spawn of the rich and famous but always feeling the very particular brand of in-it-but-not-of-it sour grapes that comes from knowing that there's always a better table and it's always for someone else.

I'd hear him bragging about Ira "constantly" being invited to swanky affairs in the Hollywood Hills to celebrate the birthdays of his dog friends whose owners were A-list machers. Of course, Sam would leave out the fact that, while our dog was attending these soirees, we sat at home or in the car, waiting to pick him up, always on the outside looking in—like Barbara Stanwyck in *Stella Dallas*. But I couldn't blame him: for a guy who spent his youth feeling like he was less than *Less Than Zero*, basking in the reflected glory of his dog's notable esteem had to feel pretty great. And it was this side of Sam, and his ability to relate to and have empathy for an animal, that began to stir in me feelings of love.

On our very first date, at a place called Berri's Cafe on Third, over a pepperoni pizza and a carafe of warm white wine, Sam recounted a reoccurring dream in which Ludwig, the mangy stray cat he'd inadvertently adopted, was in danger and he had to save him. The forms of peril in each dream changed. Sam's task, however—often risky, always impossible—remained constant: save Ludwig.

I told him about having just finished a book on Gestalt dream analysis. "The gist," I told him, "was that every part of our dreams—including animals and inanimate objects—should be viewed as projections of ourselves."

"So, what you're saying is . . . Ludwig is *me*?"

"Yeah," I said. "That's exactly right: Ludwig is you."

"And I can't be saved?"

"That I don't know," I said. "You should really be asking Ludwig—or the 'Ludwig' in your dreams . . ."

"What if I'm more into Freud?" Sam asked. "Whatever happened to 'sometimes a banana is just a banana'?"

"You'll have to ask the banana . . . ," I said, and as I did, Sam leaned in for what was to be our first-ever kiss.

Ludwig was not Sam's only sickly adoptee; he also had salvaged from the trash a half-dead houseplant he named "Bruce" by keeping him in a dark closet and watering him twice a day. When I first met Bruce, who looked like Charlie Brown's Christmas tree only worse, I thought for sure he was a goner.

"You sure he isn't dead or close to it?" I asked Sam, surveying Bruce's brittle brown leaves.

"Maybe." Sam shrugged. "But I figure he's worth a try."

We had met only a few weeks before, in a theater in East LA, where my friend Monty was appearing in a play in which Sam, on a sabbatical from law school, happened to be playing the incidental music he had also composed. I had recently been asked to sing at a nightclub and needed to hire an accompanist to go over my charts. After the performance that evening, I asked Monty to introduce me to the piano player.

"You two kids should know each other," Monty had said before running off to bum a cigarette from a fellow thespian.

"I guess we should," Sam said, eyeing me shyly as he took a swig of his Coke Classic.

What I didn't know as we stood talking that night was that this was not the first time Sam had laid eyes on me, that he had seen me from afar at a film premiere the month before. He felt compelled then to meet me, to say something, to strike up a conversation, but was alas too shy to finagle an introduction from the mutual friend with whom I happened to be speaking. So instead, he watched from a distance as I walked away toward my seat. The lights went down, and he figured that was that.

That night with Monty, when I asked Sam whether he'd play for me, he said yes so quickly I was a bit startled. When I asked him how much he'd charge me, he said he'd do it for free provided I was willing to sing a few numbers with his little jazz combo at their next gig.

"Don't you need to hear me sing first?" I asked.

"Nah," he said. "I have a hunch it'll work out."

Sam, as it turned out, would have a hunch about a lot of things, including the idea that, though I was miserable as an actress, what I'd always loved best about performing—telling stories—was not something I ever had to give up, not if *I* was the storyteller. Why idle away waiting for someone to allow me into *their* story, was the logic, when I could tell my own?

"You could write," he told me.

"I don't know how."

"Sure you do. Just write like you talk."

"Like I talk? But don't I need—"

"You just need this," he said, handing me his laptop. "And to write like you talk."

I took Sam's words to heart: much like what happens when I start talking, I started writing and couldn't stop. When I had enough material, I performed it as a solo show, which Sam helped me produce. The idea was to do this show to procure a new talent agent; instead, I ended up with a literary agent and, sometime thereafter, my first book deal.

And as for Bruce, one day not long after I first met him, he came out of the closet not only alive but robust, verdant, and flowering. Sam had never given up on Bruce, and with his encouragement I would soon learn that I had not yet given up on myself.

~

"Do you think," I asked Sam, as we cleaned up post–fluid duty, "that Ira is only stiff-upper-lipping it all for my benefit?"

Sam sighed. "All I really meant was that he can tell when you're happy and when you're not. And when you're happy, he's happy. Cuz, you know . . . he's a dog."

When you're happy, he's happy.

Simple. Lovely. If you applied these words to a human, you'd be not at all insane to feel that you were truly loved in the most beautiful, profound way possible. Did we love each other this way, Sam and I? What did we know, let alone *feel*, about each other's happiness? Was the implication that, because Ira was a dog, his concern for my contentment was not out of unadulterated love but instead out of ignorance? If he only knew better or could go to therapy, consciousness-raising sessions, or sports bars, perhaps he would somehow feel less invested in my bliss or hampered by the alternative?

When you're happy, he's happy remained long after that morning's shared chore was completed; long after we got up, walked away, and went on with our days. And in thinking about those words, I was reminded of some other ones I hadn't thought much about—not just in years but even when they were fresh:

You're the one who loves Dolly Parton.

I suppose it took ruminating on whose happiness matters—and why or why not and to whom—for me to see how my focus was perennially fucked up. Perhaps I was doomed to always hear everything as a criticism or a negative, but was that even the spirit with which it was offered? My dog having the capacity to love or to not love Dolly Parton was of little import. What mattered, as Amy had said that long-ago day with the psychic, was that he loved *me*. And I loved *him*. And this was the truth. It's been said that with a pet, you can project all your feelings, ideas, wants, needs, and dreams. In a sense, then, in loving them, maybe you are loving yourself.

~

On July 27, three weeks and three days after Jim told me Ira would likely be dead by the end of the weekend, we had a birthday party for

Ira, and all the neighbors came. I took the Bear to Gristedes so she could pick out one of those Duncan Hines cake mixes to make. Her original choice was a pink velvet cake with confetti icing, but that was just too disgusting to wrap my mind around. We settled on a still-gross-but-acceptable chocolate cake with vanilla frosting, topped with pink cake-writing gel and rainbow sprinkles.

"It was raining when Ira was sick," the Bear explained to the cashier. "But now that he's better, there's a rainbow."

We ordered pizza from Patsy's and had chips and soda and wine. We played Dolly Parton. Just before we lit the candles, Pearl, the old lady down the hall, came by with her "famous" Lipton onion-soup dip. It was the kind you just toss together with a tub of sour cream, then serve with Ruffles potato chips, but Pearl insisted hers was special.

"The secret," she whispered as she stood in the doorway, swathed in knockoff Chanel, "is mixing it all together *the day before*, then letting it sit in the fridge until you're ready to serve it." Pearl looked around to make sure the coast was clear before clutching my arm and leaning in closer. "Because when you do it this way, the soup bits get mushy and you have a properly balanced dip . . ."

"Makes sense," I said as I nodded, taking the container.

"Oh, honey, I was just telling my daughter Donna today, I said, 'Donna, I'm going to share the onion-dip recipe with Nancy—it's time.' And she said, 'Ma, you sure?' And I said, 'Absolutely. She deserves it, after the hell she's been through with that poor dog. I mean, you can't believe how bad she looks lately, and well, maybe there are other things going on—I don't know, it's none of my business—but even still, the dog and whatever went on with him, and all the money she's had to spend, because you know how expensive those New York City vets are these days. I mean, you could feed a small country for what you pay for just a checkup. But anyway, she just looks like she's been to hell and back and—' I mean, no offense, but you really did look like you'd been to hell and back—"

"Oh, please," I said, "none taken—"

"Oh, what a day it is today! What a milestone, honey—for you, for Ira! Just a few weeks ago, I was telling Donna, I said, 'Donna, you know, I just wish that poor dog could make it to his birthday later this month' (because I had it marked down on the calendar from last year, you know). And she said, 'Ma, nothing lasts forever.' And I said to her, 'I know that, but Donna, I'm going to pray!' (And I don't even pray. I mean, the last time I prayed was when George McGovern was running for president, so that oughta tell you, right?) But I said, 'I'm going to do it, Donna. I'm going to ask God (or whoever the hell is up there—Gandhi? Mother Teresa? Golda Meir?). Anyway, I'm doing it. I'm doing it. I'm praying. I'm asking, because at the end of the day it's really all you can do, right?'"

"Right," I said.

Pearl paused briefly, and, placing my hand over the bowl of dip as if it were a talisman, she stared at me for a few moments.

"So little goes the way we plan, honey, you know? But it's important to have things to believe in, even if they seem silly."

In that moment, as I stood staring into her beautiful, glassy green eyes, Pearl's beatific glow made me feel that to live amid the community of fellow travelers, weirdos, and kooks in my crumbling Chelsea apartment building was a blessing almost worth the ridiculous rent.

"Yes," I said. "More and more, I see how true that really is."

"Anyway, hon, I'm glad I told you the secret of the onion dip, cuz now my recipe will be around long after I'm gone . . ."

In the afternoon light, Pearl's skin had the translucence of a baby bird. How long, I wondered, did she have? How long did any of us have? Donna was right: nothing lasts forever. Except, of course, Pearl's onion dip, and standing there that afternoon, knowing this heartened me.

"Come on, Pearl," I said, taking her bony hand in mine. "It's time to join the party."

OCTOBER

Three

The Divine Miss O

By the fall, Ira had miraculously emerged from his tango with the Grim Reaper with what looked to be an open dance card. He was eating and had more energy and a spryness about him that almost everyone with whom he crossed paths remarked on. And yet I still found myself tiptoeing through each day, wondering how long we really had. At some point, I felt it was of the utmost importance that I not give in to the fear—rational or otherwise—that I could not save my dog; in fact, I decided that I wouldn't even entertain the possibility. I had stared down plenty of "trying times" in the past, and in those instances, there always came a moment when I located my resolve to make whatever I wanted to have happen, *happen*—a moment when I understood that my attitude and the adjusting of it was everything.

I thus found myself, as I often did in times of averted crisis, recommitting to the concept of "mindfulness." I had forgotten all about mindfulness as a thing at all, let alone a thing that I needed to traffic in on the daily, becoming one of those flagrant opportunists for whom awakening to experience occurs only when the deepest of deep shit hits the fan. It was a pattern that repeated itself quite a lot: I'd be going along in my life, blah-blah-blah, and then *boom*, out of the blue, a Bad Thing would happen. And the Bad Thing would produce, in its aftermath, a cognitive bitch slap, which would then cause me to morph, almost instantaneously, from a bored and over-it Gen Xer given to eye-rolling at anything even remotely "alternative" into a platitude-bleating Shirley MacLaine, ready to break bread with aliens. It would not even be out of character, if the situation necessitated, for me to dabble in the occult: from the time I was in my midtwenties, I'd had a long and varied relationship with a coven of witches who practiced out of an East Village Wiccan apothecary called Enchantments.

I first met the Ladies of the Coven when, after a bad breakup with a commitment-phobic jazz musician, I found myself at a party in a railroad flat near Houston Street, one of those pads where the bathroom served as a kitchen and vice versa. Desolate, I was wandering about, not knowing whether to pee or to offer to cook something, before slumping, finally, on a folding chair in the kitchen/bathroom in front of a card table that held potato chips and a roll of toilet paper. I got to talking to a girl I did not know. Gleaning that I was all manner of fucked up, the girl asked what was the matter. I described the Jazz Musician, our love and connection, further telling her that, despite his inability to commit, I was sure that we were forever soul mates and that I simply had to right the Universe's wrong and get him back.

"Have you ever been to Enchantments?" she asked. "In the East Village?"

"No," I said.

"*Go,*" she said, her eyes widening in that way that makes you know that it is the Thing You Must Do Over All Things Ever. "Just *go*. It will change your life."

This proved to be the understatement of all time.

I would go, as she instructed, for a meeting with a raven-haired witch with piercing blue eyes who sounded exactly like Fran Drescher. She would do a tarot reading for me, during which she'd point out that, while the Jazz Musician and I were indeed soul mates, there were multiple complications making our dharma painful and our continued romance all but impossible. She would send me home with a spell and a massive fire-engine-red candle, shaped like a penis, to burn until it was no more. These efforts, she said, would either bring back my Jazz Musician or rid me of him so that I could move on in peace.

"Whatevah's faw the greatest good," she assured me. "So mote it be."

I went home and did the spell as instructed, and though we remained uncoupled for the next year or so, I would periodically get together with the Jazz Musician for breakup sex until whatever was left between us burned out into a shapeless blob like that monster Dick Candle.

I will never know if the spell or the tarot reading or the candle had legs—or whether any of that is relevant, really. What was made irrefutably clear was that my initial visit and the attendant rituals utterly transformed me, and Enchantments—the place, its practitioners—became, from that moment on, comme il faut for all that bedeviled and beleaguered. Whenever life's gnarls necessitated, I would journey alone to the farthest eastern edge of Lower Manhattan—from the demise of my ill-fated romance with that rogue musician, right up to my last visit, just after Sam and I went through our first (failed) IVF when, in my attempts to get pregnant, I had become a woman obsessed.

I was willing to try anything; no curative was too zany or outrageous, and nothing—*nothing*—could stand in my way. I spent hours online in anonymous IVF chat rooms, commiserating with other faceless, fertility-hampered women with handles like "Baby4Us?" and "InvitroGirl," veering betwixt Pollyanna-ish pluck and defeatist Debbie Downerism with virtually every click of the mouse. I swilled fertility-enhancing remedies at a homeopathic joint so aggressively New Age I was sure they hadn't redecorated since the arrest of Charles Manson. I invested in acupuncture sessions with an illustrious Eastern-medicine practitioner, whose name, like the Steely Dan song, was Dr. Wu, and whose office walls were festooned with pictures of beautiful babies sprung from the loins of his patients—women, just like me, who had been, at one time, bereft of hope.

Not wanting to leave one stone unturned, I paid a visit, finally, to the witches of Enchantments. Unlike the Fran Drescher witch of my first visit eleven years prior, this new generation had assumed a somewhat more millennial sheen. Colorfully inked arms replete with perma-pentagrams, crescent moons, and yin-yang symbols sticking through sleeveless flannel shirts had replaced bodies swathed in head-to-toe black; free-spirited tendrils had been cropped into apathetic spikes; smiles had been swallowed by poker-faced miens. These chicks were *dark*. Certainly darker than the witches of yore. Oddly, though, despite this, they were even more comforting. After I had wept disconsolate tears onto what we all agreed was a decidedly enigmatic tarot card reading, they hugged me, each one offering in hushed tones their prayers for a bun in my oven. I was then sent off into the dusk with a parting gift that included a goddess bath and a custom-carved fertility candle, anointed with fragrant oils, to light on the next new moon.

Two months later, we tried IVF again. One early afternoon, after a little over a week, I pulled a home pregnancy test out of my drawer and gave it a whirl. Before I was even done peeing on the stick, two perpendicular blue lines beamed into view. *I was pregnant!* Of course, I had to pee on half a dozen more sticks before I could finally believe it was true, all the while screaming, laughing, crying—never, ever had I been more ecstatic. As wacked-out as all this sounds, just taking action and propelling myself forward made me feel less victimized—like I was doing something to turn this boat around, to make the life happen that I wanted to have. Was mine a spirituality born out of opportunism? Yes. But so what? I was taking charge of my own destiny and exercising my will.

And so it was that once Ira seemed to be stabilized, I began to open my mind, once again, to various paths of enlightenment, becoming hyperaware of what, exactly, I wanted to manifest. Meditation and positive visualization ensued. I dug out an old meditation tape Sam had bought me years before called *A Hope-Filled Mind and a Peaceful Heart*, in which this very groovy dude lulls you into this fabulously false sense of security using only his voice and a space-age-sounding synthesizer. I loved that tape; it really *did* give my mind hope and my heart peace. Every night, I would light ten white bodega candles all around the bedroom and listen while visualizing all of us happy and healthy, the candlelight circling my family like beatific fireflies dancing the hora.

When I wasn't actively trying to enlist the cosmos and the far reaches of my consciousness, my thoughts, unfettered and supple, frequently turned to Oprah Winfrey. Or, more specifically, to thematically appropriate episodes of *Oprah* in which Oprah Winfrey spoke aloud that which I needed, in any given moment, to hear. I spent a lot of time, for example, musing on the Jim Carrey episode wherein he explained to Oprah how he "law of attracted" himself a salary of $10 million for *Dumb and Dumber*. I spent even more time contemplating the episode in which J. K. Rowling explained to Oprah how we really do have the power to become what we believe (which, in her case, meant *believing* she could go from being a single mother on welfare to *becoming* the first billionaire author). But the be-all and end-all of any *Oprah* episode, as far as I was concerned, was Oprah herself. I could never, no matter whom she was chatting up, take my attention off her, especially when she was deep in Guru Oprah, get-it-gurl mode, which was often. In fact, everything on *Oprah* the show always seemed to be geared toward Oprah the lady, ferreting out, then zeroing in on the idea that if one is clear about one's intention, the Universe will bestow. There was something about the message itself, combined with Oprah's particular brand of *O*-pining, that utterly transfixed me, and soon my inner world basically became an around-the-clock *Oprah* episode.

"Be clear about your intention," I'd imagine her telling me in that sonorous baritone, "and the Universe will bestow."

These words, a benediction of sorts, encapsulated exactly what I needed to hear, and I would ingest them like a gigantic spoonful of *yes* whenever my perspective faltered or my faith floundered. It went so far that my brain would conjure the Divine Miss O—gesticulating gracefully with her hands, intoning axioms—even in the midst of the random or the mundane: I could be making the Bear's bed, cleaning the dinner dishes, or swiping my MetroCard to see how many rides I had left, and there she'd be, Oprah, smoothing my hair, lifting my chin, insisting that everything I ever needed resided in the elegant simplicity of that one little mantra.

"Darling," my British friend Zoe said after I'd recounted one afternoon at a café called Tea & Sympathy my umpteenth come-to-Oprah moment, "please know that we're all terribly delighted about dear Ira's recovery—*terribly delighted, indeed*—but (and I mean this in the best possible way) I'm afraid you've lost the plot . . ."

Perhaps so.

But, despite the tea (and the sympathy), I cared not a whit that Zoe or anyone else found my Mardi Gras of New Age embarrassments to be thoroughly wackadoo. The tyranny of my reflexive anxiety, along with my incessant fear about everything we had endured of late, lifted. I began to believe that the very reason calamity had struck was to wake me up to all that I had, and that included my marriage. So, after expressing my intent to the Universe to save my dog, I turned the focus to my husband and my yen to cultivate between us a deeper love and appreciation.

~

One weekend in October, Sam and I took a short trip to the beach with the Bear and Ira. My cousin had a house in Sagaponack, which she had generously offered to us while she was away. It was still warm enough to have dinners alfresco, so for two nights we shared spaghetti and clams for dinner and banana splits for dessert in the verdant garden under a grape arbor. After putting the Bear to bed, we'd return to the arbor to sip after-dinner wine and hash out what to do about the various issues that had been weighing on us for longer than either of us cared to admit. Our little wine bar, Ciruela, had hit a rough patch: aside from the massive difficulties of owning a food and beverage establishment in a notoriously fickle industry, other issues had cropped up of late, including an exorbitant tax increase and an evil landlord hell-bent on jacking up the rent in what was now a prime West Village location. Sam had recently let some employees go to lighten the overhead.

"I need you to take some of the shifts," he said.

I wasn't in love with this idea, I admit. I hated having to work nights after writing all day, but with the Bear just starting a new school and with my concerns for Ira, the prospect was even more daunting. That said, I was the new me—I wanted to get along, to be a better partner, to say yes more than no—so I put on my big-girl pants, took a deep breath, and agreed.

"There's something else," Sam said.

"OK . . ."

"I'm really feeling the need to spend more time focusing on my music."

This had recently become another source of contention for us: Sam, over the past year, had begun to explore the New York City singer-songwriter scene. In his spare time, he attended Greenwich Village open mics, wrote lyrics into tattered notebooks while hanging out in cafés, and began private singing lessons with an unfailingly cheerful Scottish woman who encouraged students to "risk growing into their wholeness." He began to hang out with other would-be musicians and balladeers (most of whom were still in their twenties), catching their late-night acts in Bushwick bars and trading songs back and forth on

Bandcamp. I felt he was morphing into someone new, someone who disconcertingly used terms like *awesome* for things that were frankly only so-so, someone who was suddenly referring to people as *folks* as if he'd just returned from Walton's Mountain.

It wasn't that I took particular umbrage with his wading in the shallow waters of cliché; nor did I object to his musical aspirations per se. It was that the more time he spent devoted to music, the less he spent at Ciruela, into which we had sunk, by that time, almost all our savings. We had made what, to me, was an incredibly risky investment largely so that Sam would have something to do after he quit being a lawyer, a career he despised. At the outset, I understood enough about restaurants and such to know they were not exactly a cakewalk. But Sam wanted his own business, to be his own boss. So, after much hand-wringing, I got on board, and when I did, I threw myself in whole-hog: I did everything from helping to come up with the concept and design to consulting on the menu and handling all the publicity. I took a sommelier class to learn about wine and train my palate, and I pitched in with front-of-house duties. When we opened, Ciruela was an instant success with lines out the door. People loved it. I was so incredibly proud of us. But five years had passed since Ciruela's doors had opened, and somewhere along the way, Sam had grown disenchanted with it, in much the same way he had with so many things. And though he assured me everything was under control, it seemed like every time I turned around, something was crumbling to pieces without any warning. Equipment was breaking; bills were piling up; people were quitting, or Sam was letting them go in what felt like a haphazard way. Sometimes, I would call and he wouldn't be there for several hours. When confronted, he would tell me he'd been running errands. At some point, however, he came clean and admitted he'd been at a voice lesson or a rehearsal. So, by the point at which we found ourselves, when Sam wanted to talk about music, all I could hear was alarm bells.

"What does that mean," I asked him, "'focusing on my music'?"

"It means I need time to work on my songs. I'm going to be recording them and getting ready for a gig to showcase them at the end of December."

I paused. I knew I needed to tread very carefully. We had recently been talking about adding a wine shop to our modest little empire—something we could do together as a team that would both increase revenue and be a logical extension of Ciruela. If Sam was going to be "focusing on his music," how *focused* could he be on this new venture, the prior one, or, for that matter, anything else?

"Are we still moving ahead with the wine shop?" I asked.

"Yes," he said. "What does one have to do with the other?"

"Just that it's . . . a big project—"

"Well, music is a 'big project' of mine, too," he said. "And something I want to pursue more seriously."

"More seriously as . . . ?"

"As a career."

This stopped me cold. And though he didn't utter a word, I could sense Sam challenging me to shoot down his dreams.

"Well," I began. "It seems—" My thoughts petered out; my mind began to reel. *It seems what, Nancy?* I asked myself. *What can you really say to this that's not going to cause World War III?*

What I wanted to say was *It seems like this is not the best idea. In fact, this seems like a ridiculous idea, and do you know how sick I am of having to be supportive of every insane imagining you arrive at, as though there's even a degree of merit to any of them? Do you also know how sick I am of having to use cagey language like "it seems like" so that I can at least feel good about having remained "psychologically correct" in my approach? I am not a good enough person to keep up this bullshit charade, this delicate tightrope act—in fact, I am a terrible person, because if I could tell you something real, what I would tell you is this: music is not a place for you to be placing your focus. Your focus should be on your business, which is falling apart, and your marriage, which is falling apart, and the health and well-being of your child. Music, demo tapes, voice lessons with charlatans, gigs at dumps—all of that is fine if you are keeping up with the rest of your life and the rest of your prodigious responsibilities, but, let's face it, you are* not, *about which you seem not to give even the tiniest of fucks, a stunning truth that quite frankly* terrifies *me. So, let's stop the insanity and redirect your "focus." Please, please, I beg you.*

But I didn't say any of that.

Instead, I told him very simply that I was scared.

"About Ira?" he asked.

"About our marriage," I said.

Sam looked as if something had fallen out of the grape arbor and smashed him in the head. I suppose in a way something had.

"Why—is something wrong?"

"I'm not sure. But I think we need to find out."

~

Several weeks later, Sam and I are sitting in the office of our couples therapist, Stephen, an avuncular, barrel-chested Buddhist, whose giant poached-egg eyes remind me of a benevolent Peter Lorre. It has been over a year since last we were in Stephen's office, which is a room, really, in a cluttered fourth-floor walk-up on West Fifteenth Street. We'd been seeing Stephen, our third therapist in five years, for a year and a half before abandoning our weekly sessions just shy of our tenth wedding anniversary. It wasn't intentional: I went off to do a book tour, Stephen went on a trip, and everything was left very vague as to when we would be meeting next. Time wore on, and somehow, we simply never made another appointment. The subject of a "Stephen session" would arise, but we could never seem to commit to anything tangible, and the whole thing would then quickly float away, like a little dust bunny tumbling hither and thither across an otherwise spotless parquet wood floor.

Practically, we told ourselves and each other that it was due simply to a lack of funds, and while this was certainly true—money was a major concern—secretly, I always suspected that the real "lack" we were responding to was of progress. It wasn't Stephen's fault. He was a terrific therapist—learned, funny in a highbrow-yet-groovy UC Berkeley sort of way, and certainly better than the others we'd seen. But like our marriage, though we were present—as in, actually showing up to the sessions—we were never really there, not in the way that it would matter or the way in which real change could occur. We were doing that thing where it was as if we believed that the simple act of showing up to spend a "fifty-minute hour" sitting together on an overstuffed faux-Navajo sectional sofa was enough; if magic was to occur, well, that was the exclusive domain of the magician. From time to time, we broke free of our normally passive roles and came ready to address the specific nature of our discontent. But even in those instances, the goal seemed less about protecting the collective "we" and more about proving why the other was to blame—a scenario that can be best described as "lose-lose."

Like many couples in distress, initially we went into counseling to settle a long-standing debate. For us it was, Do we move back to Los Angeles (Sam), or do we stay in New York (me)? But soon we came to see that the issue of residence was just the tipping point of many far greater issues we had been thus far unable to reconcile.

We bring Stephen up to date: the dog, his illness, the wine bar, the wine shop, our financial crisis, and then the usual things we complain about—lack of warmth, tenderness, money, sex.

Stephen is comparing love to cable television: "Not to sound glib," he says, "but like any number of promotional deals wherein you are given the first month gratis, the objective is to entice you, and once you're hooked, you pay."

As he speaks, Stephen rolls his gold fountain pen between his thumb and index finger. It is a gesture he does with such frequency that I have often wondered if perhaps the pen-rolling acts as a sort of

Aladdin's lamp from which thoughts and bons mots emanate in an endless, clever stream.

Sam and I, for the first time in forever, as we sit there next to each other in Stephen's room, are holding hands. It happened unconsciously, reflexively, the way it always used to. I take this as a sign that finally—finally—we are here to really do the work.

"Paying's cool," Sam chuckles, squeezing my hand. "As long as you feel like you're getting a return on your investment . . ."

I laugh, though I don't really get the joke. I'm an easy laugh—perhaps too easy. Stephen laughs, too, and when he does, his shoulders bounce up and down while, at the same time, he clutches against his lap the little brown leather notebook into which he occasionally jots tiny shrink hieroglyphics. I am feeling a great sense of purpose all of a sudden; I feel serious, studious, wanting badly to learn, to solve, to fix. On another day, at another time, the yukking it up could easily have pissed me off, and yet, on this day, I say nothing, choosing instead to momentarily shift focus to the decor of Stephen's office. Aside from the faux-Navajo sectional, the furnishings, doubtlessly picked up at flea markets and tag sales, are few. There's a wood desk pushed up against the wall between two dusty windows and a small, slightly bent kidney-shaped coffee table that sits between the couch and Stephen's shrink chair. The usually wheezing furnace is silent on this late-October morning. The mismatched midcentury tchotchkes, with their flat, muted earth tones, remind me of so many of our previous sessions and the pallid days that followed, where, despite our best efforts, we simply could not move past the things we could never seem to move past.

I wonder, briefly, if it is by conscious design that the overarching theme of the room's palette suggests muddiness, entrenchment, something needing to be worked through? Or am I once again projecting my own state of being onto my surroundings? *Isn't it just as possible an interpretation,* I think to myself, *that these hues convey a certain rootedness, encouraging the dwellers herein to remain grounded and forthright and avoid flight?* I am not sure to what I should attribute the fact that, despite my resolve, I find myself more restless than usual in Stephen's room or my growing concern that this setting is perhaps better suited to the pastoral poetry Stephen composes in his downtime, when he isn't ministering to unhappy couples, who almost always arrive when it's much too late.

Stephen is now saying that love will almost inevitably lead to disappointment.

"The challenge," he says, "is how to live a good life in spite of that."

I get it, I think to myself. *And I want this—to live a good life in spite of the inevitability of disappointment. I want to face it all head-on—to be real and to deal.*

"Things have been not good for a long time," I begin, and though I feel positive about the fact that we are here and addressing our stuff, I am suddenly overcome, and tears I had not been anticipating begin to fall down my cheeks. "I . . . I'm sorry . . ."

Sam takes over, explaining that in addition to the usual issues that still plague us, the latest is that he would like to pursue his dream of becoming a singer-songwriter and that I am negative about this idea.

"Nancy thinks that it will get in the way of our new wine shop—"

"I guess I just don't get how there'll be time—"

"I need to pursue my music—it's my passion—"

"OK, but it just doesn't make sense."

"Makes all the sense in the world. To *me*, anyway."

"OK, so explain it to me—I want to know what you're thinking, like, what's the plan—"

"How can you even *question me* or *this* when I have always supported your dreams?" Sam says, turning to face me. *"How?"*

"I think," Stephen says, jumping in, "what Nancy might be responding to—and correct me if I'm wrong, Nancy—is that she may not trust this as a genuine pursuit for you, because in the past you have wanted her to get on board about something—be it you becoming a documentary filmmaker or the idea you had with the T-shirts or the one where you wanted to sell . . . water, I think it was . . . Anyway, not important, and then—whatever it was—it didn't stick for you. Is that more or less what you're trying to say, Nancy? That this is about trust for you—you needing to trust that this is real?"

"Well," I say, "that was certainly an issue in the past, yes, but this . . . I mean, the fact is that at this point we have two businesses and a family—a child—who we need to remember in all of this."

"I understand." Stephen nods.

"This is bullshit," Sam tells Stephen flatly. "You are *always* on her side."

Stephen looks stunned; Sam continues, now addressing me.

"So, I should go back to being a lawyer and just be fucking miserable, right?"

"What?" I say. "*No one* is saying you should be a lawyer again. Where is that even coming from? I just don't see how we sink money—money we don't even have—into—"

"But you're perfectly happy to throw money at the vet—"

"Throw money at—?"

"To the tune of four grand—"

"OK, that was for our dog—*our* dog. *Ours,* not yours or mine—ours."

"And I'm supposed to be on board with whatever *you* want to spend money on?"

"How is this even comparable? Also, it's not like I set out to spend four grand. Are you saying I shouldn't have tried saving Ira? I mean, how could I not try?"

"It's excessive. And inhumane."

"Guys—" Stephen says, jumping in.

"I see. But doing absolutely nothing while he suffers and then dies on the floor of our closet is humane?"

"If we lived on a farm, we'd let nature take its course."

"Guys—"

"On a farm?"

"Yes—that's how they do it, and it's beautiful."

"What the fuck do you know of farm living?"

"Guys!" Stephen bellows. "Enough!"

I am somehow filled with remorse and at the same time impressed with our fight-game. It takes a special brand of asshole to piss off a Buddhist, and we are definitely in this moment those assholes. Having retreated to opposite corners of the faux-Navajo sectional, our hands now rest in our own laps. Sam glances at me briefly, then turns his attention to the dusty windows.

After a minute or two of letting the vibe cool, Stephen speaks. "Look, you two—what's happening here, what you are both responding to is *scarcity.* 'I' has replaced 'we,' and what we are left with is the feeling of *scarcity.* He wants sex; she's not in the mood. He wants to live in LA; she wants to live in New York. She wants to invest in a home; he wants to invest in a business. She wants to do whatever it takes to save the dog; he feels that it's unfair and that they should let him go; she is upset that it seems he is giving up without a fight. And so on. So, what happens when we are in a love relationship and we find ourselves no longer united as "one" but instead two opposing forces, duking it out, feeling hopeless, mourning the loss of abundance? Well, you have two choices: one, you pick up your toys and leave the sandbox, dissolving ties, ending the marriage. Or . . ." Stephen stops, tosses his notebook onto the bent kidney-shaped coffee table between us, and leans forward. "You look at the gift that this all is and begin to initiate the act of real loving."

Hours later, I am home, lying on the bed. The Bear lies next to me, sleeping; Ira lies next to her, doing the same. They are both snoring softly. Sam is out. The ten bodega candles are around us but remain unlit, and I cannot muster either the energy or the concentration to listen to my meditation tape. Instead, I lie staring at the ceiling and think of Oprah. I imagine her blinking her eyes real slow in that way that lets you know she's more than a tad over your shit.

Her dulcet tones pierce the quiet: *Did you hear him?* she says. *Look at the* gift, *girl. Look at the* gift. *Now, what was that again about being clear about your intention?*

And I was, I tell her telepathically. *I was clear. But then . . . I dunno what happened.*

Ego happened, girl. Ego happened.

My ego, I ask, *or his?*

Gurl. Come now.

OK, so it's me?

The shit between you? No. But I'm not dealing with that. I'm asking you to leave your ego at the door. State your intention and be clear, and you will receive the support you need. Remember?

And this singer-songwriter crap? I ask. *What about that?*

Maybe you should try letting go. Maybe you should try letting go of the expectation or the need to "get," and simply try to give. Sam needs you to help at the wine bar? Do it. Sam wants time to devote to his singer-songwriter stuff? Give it. Give, and give freely. Be generous. Stop giving a shit about being right all the time—just stop. It doesn't really matter if you believe that his becoming a troubadour at the age of forty-three is doable or even appropriate for a grown-ass man with a family; if your man wants to become the next Kenny Loggins, who are you to stand in his way?

I realize that this "Oprah," the one of Kenny Loggins references, is a fraud; this "Oprah" is "Faux-Prah." But perhaps there is still something to be gleaned from her; perhaps there is something to my just sucking it up and letting go of my need to fix, to change, to win. Isn't the point, after all, to reconnect, to recommit, to revitalize what once was? I decide to send Sam an email, in which I will tell him that I am on his side, that

I am with him and love him, that I will work the Ciruela shifts, and that I look forward to cheering him on when he performs his new songs. But as I leave the bedroom to get my computer, it occurs to me that all the intentions in the world mean nothing if both partners in a marriage are not on board. The intentions need to be said not just clearly but also genuinely to each other, and then maybe the Universe will follow. Even if I want these things, does Sam? And if so, how much? And as I open my laptop, I see an email from Sam, the subject of which is "A New Leaf."

> I want to work on this. If something is broken, then I want to repair it. I think the wine store is going to be great for us, and I will not drop the ball—I promise. Music has given me a way to express myself, and that makes the world a different place for me. But you are important, our life together is important. If I have been deaf before, I hear you now. I want this, I want you.

Maybe the Universe really had heard me. More importantly, so had my husband. And for the moment, this was enough; for the moment, I felt like every one of those solicitous midwesterners in Oprah's audience when they learned they'd be leaving her studio with a *"new carrr!"* But I was leaving with something better: a hope-filled mind. In as stealth a way as possible, so as not to disturb my snoring Bear and beagle, I crawled off the bed and lit all ten bodega candles. It was amazing to see them all ablaze, knowing that this would be the last time they'd all be the exact same size, their flames so completely in sync. By morning, they'd be so much lower; some of them might even have burned out. If there had been a way to press pause, I'd have done it.

Instead, I just stood for a while, staring into the glow.

NOVEMBER

Four

Bliss Balls

As Ira's condition continued to stabilize, so, too, did our marriage. Stephen, with whom we'd had only a few sessions, had to leave town and would be gone until early spring. This concerned me—what would become of us now without our Obi-Wan Kenobi? In the weeks that followed his departure, a strange calm came over Sam and me; there was no fighting or conflict in the way that there might have been in our recent past, but no passion, connection, or exchange, either. Instead, a sense of order evolved, and with it came an almost formal politeness, more than I had seen us have toward each other in years. It wasn't tenderness, the kind of gentle respect with which partners or people who love each other deeply accord each other. It was something else entirely, and it was this quality of courteousness—genteel, effusive— that I found so terribly disconcerting.

I remembered noticing in couples on the brink of breaking up a level of exasperation in which everything was suddenly uncontained: their hostility toward each other, their squabbles at one time experienced only privately, now bleeding out at social events. These were not couples for whom brawling was a form of foreplay, like Liz Taylor and Richard Burton, who screamed at each other daily but not necessarily with malice or intent to inflict wounds—screaming merely as a style of relating. I'm referring to people who would have been appalled to have their private conflicts play out like those of bratty movie stars on a bender. Caught in that place wherein they were trying to maintain the appearance of a "functioning marriage," they'd have no awareness that the jig was up and the only people who didn't get it were them. And as I pondered this previously arrived-at philosophical tipping point, my thoughts turned to my latest bout of unease: Were there, I wondered, people who weren't openly horrid to each other but instead whose dying relationship became warmer, more "functioning" than it had been in years, just before the final coup, like some sort of eerie calm before the deluge?

One bright November morning, as I was just waking up, Sam stood at the foot of our bed, holding a cup of coffee in one hand and a pamphlet in the other.

"Bliss Balls," he said, grinning.

"I'm sorry?"

"Bliss Balls," he repeated, shaking the pamphlet at me. "That's the answer."

"To what question?" I asked, propping myself up on a pillow.

"To Stephen being on the lam. Here," he said, handing me the coffee and the pamphlet, which advertised a series of New Age "Love Seminars," the upshot of which was this: an herbalist from New Paltz named Karen, whose immensely popular practice existed "to re-weave the healing cloak of the Ancients," conducted various wellness workshops heavily attended by the stressed and beleaguered denizens of New York City. Things like Costa Rican restorative aura adventures, bimonthly shamanic weed walks, or just a simple "Day Devoted to Trees." The seminar Sam had circled was a one-day-only couples' event in "Love Medicine" to be held at the Open Center on Spring Street in

Soho. After sitting together on *zafu* cushions while Karen led a guided group meditation, couples would then make (and feed each other) holistic aphrodisiacs derived from special herbs and chocolate, a.k.a. "Bliss Balls." It was both an activity *and* a parting gift, and each couple was to be sent home with their very own "Balls" to enjoy until the supply (or the couple, I suppose) was exhausted.

Seriously—what was not to love about any of this?

Especially the part where my normally very dry and decidedly un-woo-woo hubby was pitching it? I was *so in.*

On the evening of the seminar, after a (calm, disconcertingly polite) dinner at Spring Street Natural, we made our way over to the Open Center to "reclaim the intimacy and passion" that eluded us.

This was problematic for several reasons.

For one thing, even in the beginning, Sam and I never had the sort of frenzied, unbridled, rip-off-your-clothes-and-fuck-me-now kind of love affair I envisioned the other Love Seminar participants to have once enjoyed. People who trafficked in shamanic weed walks surely would be able to, without much prodding, *get down.* Which brings me to the second problem: Sam and I hadn't had sex in several years.

Several.

Years.

I knew people who complained they had "no sex" but meant they had it only once a week or once, even, every two weeks. But Sam and I, again, hadn't had sex in several years. I knew, for his part, Sam attributed the coital wasteland to me—which wasn't without merit, since he would have been happy to get it on if I were game, which I was not. The question was, Why?

Theories were bandied about: Maybe it was because I'd slutted around so much in my freewheeling youth that now I was compensating by "overcorrecting." Maybe being a mom was the culprit, and I was viewing myself through Madonna-whore-colored glasses. Maybe so much had gone down over the years that, by the time we were signing up for seduction seminars with hippies, I was so over sex I (literally) had no fucks left to give.

Maybe it was hormonal.

Maybe it was thyroidal.

Maybe it was emotional.

Maybe it was mental.

Maybe it was all of the above.

Maybe.

Whatever the reason, the more it persisted—the more time wore on—the worse I felt about it. I tried to figure out what to do: I went online and read articles by sexperts, all of whom unanimously subscribed to a philosophy best described as "fuck first, ask questions later." Stop discussing, they all beseeched; stop dissecting, and simply . . . *dive in*. It was a novel approach, and Sam for one was enthusiastic about the concept of less chatting. So dive we did, and lo and behold . . . it worked.

Or it worked once.

"The key to doing it is just to do it," I remember telling Sam afterward as we lay in each other's arms. "We just have to say that this is something we're committed to doing, right?"

"Right." He nodded.

And as we lay there, spent and content, I truly thought we'd made it over the hump. But our big opening night was also our closing night, and in the three years since that valiant attempt, we'd never tried the old throwing-caution-to-the-wind routine again. Did we discuss it? I don't remember. I know I thought about it. But I never made it past the realm of thought, because something stopped me—I don't know what. Maybe past resentments? Unreleased rage? Not being particularly turned on? Who knows. But no matter how hard I tried, I could neither open myself to his advances nor make any overtures of my own. It's funny how, in all the time I spent examining this issue, I never wondered why

I found it so easy to shoulder the blame for our "lack in the sack" or why it never occurred to me that maybe it took two to *not* tango.

Standing there, waiting for the Open Center's elevator to lift us out of our marital malaise and into Nirvana, I wondered just how this Karen chick could possibly help Sam and me and how we were supposed to "get back" that which never was.

Fanning ourselves two by two across the vast loft space, we settled onto colorful Mexican blankets and lavender-infused *zafus*. I scanned the faces of the other couples, all so hopeful to recover their collective mojos. Were these people who had at one time been crazy in love, unable to contain their lust for each other, who had simply after many years of togetherness hit a snag in the road and merely needed a gentle nudge? Or was the bloom even further off the rose, and they had become so devoid of amorous feeling for each other that they were unable to recall what had drawn them together in the first place? These were the things that coursed through the mind Karen had urged me to turn off during the guided meditation portion so that I could "cultivate unconditional friendliness of thought."

I lay back, listening to Karen, whose voice—sweet, feminine, like it had taken the teensiest combo hit of helium and weed—sounded incredibly familiar. *Stevie Nicks,* I thought to myself. *This Karen chick sounds like a dead ringer for Stevie Nicks. How great would* that *be,* I thought, *if it really* was *Stevie, and the future of my sex life could be in the hands of a woman whose use of a metaphor is as peerless as her ability to rock a granny shawl?* Sinking deeper into my *zafu,* I found myself suddenly much more willing to be taken on a make-believe journey through space and time by pretending that our fearless leader was the person I consider to be the greatest part of Fleetwood Mac. *This is OK,* I told myself. *Whatever it takes.* And as Karen/Stevie began to ferry us through imaginary rain forests and golden deserts brimming with rosy blooms that somehow stayed alive even though they existed in a desert, I was finally able to unclench and just . . . be.

I feel myself growing sad and guilty, weighed down by the belief that our sex problems are all my fault. Once upon a time, I never could have imagined becoming the sort of woman who would pray to God her husband didn't put the moves on, or who would stall forays into the boudoir by yammering on and on and on about endless bullshit so he'd tire and give up before even attempting. For many years, sex and the having of it had been as natural to me as ice cream on a hot day. It made me feel alive in a way that few things did and had frankly been a huge part of every relationship I'd had since I was a freewheeling New York University coed. During my twenties, one might have described me as "an easy lay," and not only would I have been inclined to agree with this assessment, it would have made me glad. But by the time I met Sam, I was thirty-one and had been to therapy and been burned in enough relationships to realize that sex had more often than not been a diversion—from my growth both as a woman and as a human being, and most significantly, from the deep connection I truly craved. I began feeling empty and alone with every fleeting encounter: I wanted more, needed more, deserved more. With Sam, I felt there was the possibility of this "something more" that I sought—that ours was a romance built on a different sort of rapport, the kind that is grown-up and settled. We talked—really, really talked. We laughed—really, really laughed. So maybe the earth didn't move—what we had, I told myself, was something better and more enduring.

I think of Sam and I having heart-to-hearts about the absence of sex in our marriage. He is patient, introspective, never raising his voice. We speak about it intellectually, clinically, and I remember these conversations only in fragments, as if they took place in the midst of an accident, so piecing them together presents a retrospective challenge. But what I remember most when I remember anything is the subject of my "frigidity." I remember hearing this word and feeling as if my entire being had been body-snatched, and in its place some sort of wan-looking Victorian lady in a pale cotton nightgown had been inserted.

Karen speaks; I zone out further, hopscotching through my sexual history, and each time I land on the square marked "frigid," I am confused.

If I was really frigid, was there a way to explain the passionate sex I had with Sam in my dreams?

"She's longing for you," Stephen would point out as I tearfully recounted yet another one of these unconscious sexcapades. "Are you hearing this?"

"I'm *hearing* it." Sam would shrug. "But I'm not seeing it. Or feeling it. And isn't that the problem?"

This was true—he was not. I could never seem to untangle it when I was awake. But if my sexuality was a thing of the past, why did I find myself not just dreaming of my husband but fantasizing about other men? Why, then, would I become attracted to other men, in one case so deeply that what began as somewhat flirty but nevertheless harmless email exchanges blossomed into a full-blown emotional affair that threatened to derail two marriages before I abruptly ended all communication?

What we have, I had told myself about Sam and me when we were new, *is something better . . . Ours is a romance built on a different sort of rapport.*

I'm not sure why I thought that having a mature, stable partnership and having hot sex were mutually exclusive, or that hot sex and the having of it wasn't something I would eventually really miss. But lying on my *zafu*, thinking about all these things while a woman who sounds like one of my feminist heroes tries to oil the rusted-over parts of my heart, all I can think is how much I want this all to work, how very badly I want and need my husband.

~

"OK, lovers," Karen intoned as she began to pass out ingredients bundled in sari fabric and tied together with twine. "Gather around the cauldron!"

Two by two, we went up to stir the pot, then spoon the mixed and melted fudgy liquid into individual round molds for the final touches. There was great ceremony to each couple's cauldron moments, mostly because Karen asked that while stirring we look deeply into each other's eyes. And it was in that precise moment, when Sam and I were forced to look at each other over a bubbling pot of high-grade Valrhona chocolate and horny goat weed, that I learned what it was that we might rescue from days gone by: laughter. Suddenly and without any warning whatsoever, we were irrevocably overcome with hysterical laughter. And this laughter continued unabated as we fed each other Bliss Balls, after we got home with our parting gift of Bliss Balls, and whenever one or the other of us simply invoked the words *bliss* or *balls*.

For weeks to come, when we weren't dining in on Bliss Balls, we were dining out on the tale of how a foray into the wild and woolly world of New Age bromides made us remember ourselves. Maybe ingesting Bliss Balls didn't transform our sex life, or even so much as make a dent, but we were nevertheless buoyed by the belief that no matter what had shifted in the eleven and a half years of our marriage, we still found the very same things hilarious. And "in the stillness of remembering what we had and what we lost," this, at least to me and for the moment, meant everything.

Five

A House Is Not a Home

The Bliss Balls, for all their lack of legitimate potency, served as a curative balm that began coursing its way through numerous parts of our lives. Or at least the episode itself did. Suddenly, everything was exciting and ripe with possibility. Just a few weeks after attending the Love Seminar, we finalized the deal to assume ownership of the sweet little wine shop to run in tandem with Ciruela. Pre–Bliss Balls, things had been in a constant state of flux: first, we didn't think we'd have the money to put down; then we did; then the owner decided he didn't want to sell; then he suddenly decided he did; then he circled back once again to not so sure.

One day, Sam and I were walking around the Village, talking about what to do next, what with all the owner's hemming and hawing. It occurred to me we were not far from the shop, and suddenly, I had the urge to visit.

"Why?" Sam asked.

"Dunno." I shrugged. "Just a feeling. I just feel like we should."

"Why?" Sam repeated. "We're not his friends—he barely knows us!"

"Well, maybe that's the problem," I said, pulling him across Seventh Avenue.

I knew that the owner—a middle-aged Village hippie—had been a longtime bachelor who, just six months prior to our dealings with him, had married one of his much younger customers after learning he'd knocked her up. As soon as she popped the kid out, the wife, like so many mothers of newborns, realized she was over the city and over apartment living. She insisted not only that they hightail it to the Berkshires, where they had a little cottage next to a creek, but that her hubby sell his beloved wine shop and retire to a life as a househusband, where she could keep an eye on his wandering ones. Though, outwardly, the wine shop owner presented joy about his newfangled domesticity, I didn't quite buy it. Maybe it was that he winced a little when he spoke of the wedded bliss his life would soon be, living with this beautiful woman and their baby in all that glorious country air. Perhaps, like any hippie worth his weight in ganja, he was at least open to life's new adventures. But my gut told me that his ambivalence about selling the shop had everything to do with what letting go of it symbolized: his youth and his freedom and, let's face it, all that readily available poontang. I don't know whether it was all those weird herbs or the high-grade chocolate, but my intuition was unusually keen, being governed almost exclusively by emotional versus rational logic. *Visit him,* the voice in my head kept saying. *It will be good.*

~

For the next few hours, Sam and I hung out with the owner. As customers streamed in and out and the afternoon sun shifted its gaze, dappling the many wine bottles that lined the brick walls, we dove deep into madcap conversation. Things like the difference between destiny and fate, the difference between dry and "off-dry" wines, and the fact that in the late 1980s I danced in a cage at a nightclub called Mars.

I'm not sure which of these heady subjects did the trick, but by the end of the discussion the owner was ready to sell.

One rainy day, after signing all the paperwork, Sam and I sat together in the shop, sharing a bottle of Lambrusco and a pepperoni pizza from John's of Bleecker Street, and to the strains of John Lennon's *Double Fantasy*, we made out for the first time in forever. Perhaps a cannier person would have been put off by the record Sam chose to play that rainy afternoon. And not just because the album was Lennon's last before his untimely demise but also because there was portent in its marking the tragic end of a glamorous love affair. My feelings, instead, were imbued with the ambient fantasy of *Double Fantasy*—to be lovers and partners for whom, like John and Yoko, there could never be another. I felt distinctly light that day, sanguine and unfettered about our future, like we might be shifting once again—only this time toward each other rather than apart.

Later, after picking the Bear up from a playdate, I brought her back to the shop, and we danced en famille to Sly and the Family Stone until way past all our bedtimes. The rain had stopped, but the air was still moist by the time we pulled down the metal gate and locked up, and when we piled into a taxi with our sleeping Bear, I slid up against Sam and laid my head on his shoulder.

"Some rainy days are the sunniest," I said.

"I love you," he said.

I looked at him. *He means it,* I thought. *Now more than ever.*

"I love you, too."

~

It was only a few days after our day of *Double Fantasy* and dancing to the Family Stone that I walked into our apartment and noticed, I mean *really noticed*, how shittily we had been living. There were only two rooms aside from the kitchen and bath, and still, I must have spent at least an hour floating between them, totally stunned, both at what I was seeing and how, up to that moment, it had all eluded me. Makeshift, dumpy—if a stranger happened upon the joint, they'd more than likely come to the conclusion that it was the domain of either squatters of little means or bandits on the run. *What is the rhyme? What is the reason?* I kept thinking as I stood, mouth agape, scanning the "decor" that might best be described as "early unfinished business." The living room alone was haphazardly furnished and arbitrarily organized: a Deco dry bar here, a way-too-big-for-the-space electric piano there, a tattered and stained light-blue stuffed whale-rocker from FAO Schwarz plopped in the center of a tastefully muted Persian rug, fraying IKEA chairs strewn around a fake Saarinen dining table wedged into a corner.

Granted, the apartment itself was never meant to be a place to live; it had been a place to perch until we could find something permanent. Six years later, "being there momentarily" was the only part of that narrative we agreed upon. Sam had assumed we'd wing our way back to Los Angeles after the Bear was born, because that's where he was from, where his parents and siblings were, and where we had been for the first three years of our marriage. I, on the other hand, had been under the impression that we were staying in New York City, where *I* was from, where we were *now*, and where I thought we *should* be. So the lack of thought—the complete and utter disregard even for the design or decoration of our abode—owed a great deal to this very specific tug-of-war: we were neither here nor there, because one or the other refused to be there or here.

Prior to signing what was to be only a one-year lease on this overpriced one-bedroom rental, we had been living for two years on another lily pad of sorts, in the form of an open loft in a former box-cutting factory in the Meatpacking District. We had landed *there* after moving east from Los Angeles. For twenty-four months, we had looked for an apartment to buy, coming close on several occasions. But for this reason or that, it never happened, and we ended up staying. Then I got pregnant, and suddenly the loft lost its luster of cool. I desperately wanted something less bohemian, something with walls, even if there was only one. I remembered hearing, years before, of a prewar, red-brick behemoth populated by gay men, divorcées, and many, many dogs that took up two entire avenue blocks in deepest Chelsea. It had character, a storied past, and decent security. One Sunday, in my first trimester, I wended my way alone up Ninth Avenue to the leasing office, where I was told there was a unit on the tenth floor. I swanned around the living room and bedroom, digging the vibe, then walked into the bathroom and looked out the window, where I saw the Empire State Building. I stood gazing at it for a few moments, unable to turn away.

"Any questions?" asked the leasing agent.

"Just one," I replied, still staring out the window. "How soon can we move in?"

There would be many times over the next seven years and beyond that I would find myself in that very same spot, eyes fixed north toward those 102 glorious Art Deco stories. Sometimes, it would be during the day, when the silvery structure's steeple looked like the finger of God or someone equally fabulous, deferring all queries to the heavens. Other times, I faced a facade emblazoned with color, thematic, occasionally campy, etched in perpendicular glory amid an inky sky. I would often make a game of guessing the color before I looked out the window, and if I was correct, which was a rarity, I'd take it as a positive omen. More often than not, however, I simply decided that whatever color it happened to be made perfect cosmic sense (*It's green because I bought a plant / made money / ate a salad for lunch!*).

The Chelsea apartment was not the first place we had lived with a view of an iconic structure, nor was it the first time a move was precipitated by the addition of a new family member. As newlyweds in Los Angeles, Sam and I had lived for a year in a Normandy-style apartment complex in the Fairfax District, right down the street from El Coyote, the kitschy Mexican restaurant where Sharon Tate ate her last enchilada. It was a beautifully maintained two-bedroom pad, built in the twenties, with a Juliet balcony from which, on smogless days, you could see the Hollywood sign. Like the Chelsea apartment, it, too, was a building of many dogs: There was the Akita who lived right below us with the lesbian couple whose middle-of-the-night fights were often so violent and fraught with invective that I was sure one day we'd awaken to an O. J.–style crime scene. There were also a German couple with a crippled labradoodle they wheeled around in a Maclaren baby stroller; a gay film executive with a French bulldog he named Stella Stevens, after the actress who played the hooker married to Ernest Borgnine in *The Poseidon Adventure*; and a black chick whose Pomeranian barked incessantly and lunged at anyone wearing flip-flops. What with all the dogs on the premises of our decidedly dog-friendly building, it never occurred to us that we'd run into a snafu with Mr. Silverman, our gruff Orthodox landlord.

"Mazel tov," Silverman said when I picked up the phone a few days after we brought Ira home. "I hear you two have a new puppy."

"Yes," I said. "He's adorable. We named him Ira."

"Ira," Silverman chuckled. "I had an uncle named Ira."

"Aww!"

"Yes, *alava shalom* . . . he's gone many years now . . ."

"Oh, I'm so sorry."

"And I'm afraid your Ira will be gone soon, too."

"I'm . . . sorry?"

"You're sorry a lot. And now *I'm* sorry, too. You see, I don't allow beagles."

Silverman, as it turned out, was a breedist. Either Ira had to go, or we all did.

Sam went over our lease with a fine-tooth comb and, finding no clause that prevented beagles (or any breed, for that matter), tried to use legal reason. But Silverman, kicking it old-school, would have none of it.

"Sorry, *boychik*," Silverman said as he hammered the stake with the FOR RENT sign into the grassy knoll in front. "But I answer to my own authority, *Baruch Hashem* . . ."

Before Silverman finally let us out of our lease—minus the security deposit, for which we did not have the energy to fight—we began a frantic search for other apartments. In the paper one day, I found not an apartment to rent but a house for sale in neighboring Hancock Park. It seemed impossibly fabulous: a 1923 barrel-vaulted-ceiling Spanish colonial. Birds of paradise waved languidly from outside every window; honeysuckle dangled from the terra-cotta-tiled roof. There were three bedrooms, two baths, and arched doorways leading to a tiled loggia surrounded by a lush garden with ten varieties of roses and a stone fountain. The air was thick with night-blooming jasmine. It needed work, but even still, it was affordable, and I could see us being happy there. We made an offer; it was accepted, and suddenly a nightmare situation had turned into a dream.

For the next almost two years, this magical abode's three inhabitants enjoyed the very best of indoor-outdoor California living: as day spilled into night, the humans wined and dined alfresco, while the canine resident frolicked in the garden's grass—racing around it, rolling in it, masking his scent to foil imaginary rabbits. I thought we'd never leave.

And then, one day, we did. We said goodbye to the loggia and the archways and the jasmine and the wonderful walls that held us in a way no other residence ever again would. I never quite understood how or why we decided to leave, or why, at the very least, we decided on selling versus renting. There had been an opportunity to move to New York, the basis of which was flimsy, yet Sam still felt strongly that it was time for a change. "You'll be much happier in New York," he said, and I couldn't really argue with that, because I knew it was true. I was unhappy pursuing an acting career that made me feel endlessly demoralized, even when I was working.

Then the World Trade Center was destroyed; I was beside myself with grief over what had happened to my beloved city and over the loss of a dear friend in the towers. My survivor's guilt writ large, I kept thinking I should be there, with the other downtowners, helping somehow. But still, when I thought of leaving—really saying goodbye to our house and Los Angeles and the lifestyle I may not have adored but had grown accustomed to—I was totally wrecked. I don't know that I ever could have brought myself to leave, truly, had Sam not insisted, for which I was later grateful, and for which he later held me accountable.

Thus, the move became a major source of contention between us, and we could never agree on why we decided to leave. Feelings of melancholy about the matter would arise but then be quickly replaced by more hardy ones of mutual resentment. A day would arrive many years later when I would look back on it—the house, the story of the house—and find it almost impossible to believe that it had ever been. That we'd ever lived and loved in a place like that house at all, our very own Brigadoon, existing out of place and out of time, then gone, just like that, in a single poof.

Awash in my various remembrances of things past, I gathered Ira up in my arms, took him over to the sofa, and fed him his various meds, smooshing the pills into some hamburger meat, then placing the balled-up mixture on the very back of his tongue. I shut his snout like a Pez dispenser and kissed his nose until I felt him swallow. After the meds were administered, he lay next to me, rhythmically licking the lock of Kewpie-doll hair on his privates until rolling, finally, onto his back, offering up his belly for me to rub. Sinking into the back of the sofa, I did just that while once again looking around the room at the furniture, rugs, artwork, tchotchkes—silently recounting *The Story of Us* from the vantage point of each and every item. The pair of Chinese marble tables were purchased at that antique place in Santa Barbara, the one into which we stumbled while talking about names for our future children. On top of one of those Chinese tables stood the ceramic Venetian gondolier we got in Ventura—the one with the broken toes that was supposed to be a lamp. But we could never figure out what color lampshade to get, so we never bothered to even turn him on (the double entendre of which amused us both to no end).

I don't know how long I sat there, cataloguing our belongings and their stories within our story, but at some point, I turned my attention back to Ira and his splayed-wide-open hind legs and belly, which I continued to rub, occasionally catching soft strands of white hair between my fingers. He was so tired that his eyes barely fluttered when the sofa groaned under my shifting weight, yet another sign of dilapidation that until right then had escaped me. That sofa was the first big purchase we had made for our newlywed pad, and we had brought it home just a few months before Ira. It was such a to-do, going back and forth between the ubiquitous overstuffed shabby-chic model and the more streamlined version, but we ultimately chose the latter because it was also a sleeper. The original slipcover, long gone, had a muted poinsettia print, very early 1950s, like something out of Kim Basinger's house in *L.A. Confidential*. Over the course of eleven years, the sofa had known so many incarnations, looks, and patterns, and had been tucked into a second bedroom, an office, and finally a living room. Which fabric was it when we were the happiest?

After the *L.A. Confidential* slipcover came the much-yearned-for leopard-print one, custom-made from a durable and soft cotton blend found somewhere on La Brea Avenue. I'd dreamed of having a leopard sofa, dreamed of it taking center stage in a living room painted a bright, lacquered red, almost like the one Diana Vreeland had in her famed New York apartment. My leopard sofa, on the other hand, was in a tiny room in our Spanish colonial house that was both a den where we watched TV and my office, where I wrote at a vintage Heywood-Wakefield rattan desk. Sam and I spent so many hours curled up together on the sofa's leopard incarnation, watching award shows or movies like *Double Indemnity* or the terrifying and bleak footage of September 11. Whenever we wanted to talk about whatever we wanted to talk about, we for some reason always ended up in that room, the tiniest in the house, on that sofa with its uniquely plush fabric. Then we moved east; the Meatpacking loft came furnished, so I removed the leopard-print slipcover, folded it up, and sent it, the sofa, and the rest of our belongings to storage.

For reasons I can't explain, when we finally collected our things—the sofa included—to furnish the Chelsea apartment, I found a premade flax-colored linen thing at Bed Bath & Beyond to cover the sofa instead of that fabulous leopard-print one. Somehow, my vision for us no longer included the liveliness of leopard print. The sofa became a place to park and think, a place to chill with the Bear while she watched her beloved Rodgers and Hammerstein musicals, a place to sleep when we were fighting, a place to pet my sick dog while I traveled in my mind back to happier days. Even in its neutral-colored mundaneness, it still yielded significance as the first place I sat (when I could finally sit anywhere at all) after I came home from the hospital post-C-section, the place where I would breast-feed my baby while watching the leaves bloom, then turn from green to gold to brown, before finally disappearing entirely from the red brick across the courtyard.

But it was not until the Bear became a preschooler that the sofa assumed its most crucial latter-day role, becoming the setting of and the gateway to a fiction curated for the benefit of those most onerous of looky-loos, Other Moms.

One evening, at a girls'-night-out "bonding" dinner with the moms from the Bear's preschool, the subject turned to conjugal relations and the issues of finding privacy in small apartments shared with young children. Though I hadn't much in common with these women, save for our kids attending the same pre-K, they were fun, and there were benefits to having "mom friends." There's a particular loneliness that comes with motherhood that can make you yearn for even the wispiest of connections, if only to say that you did something social that day with another adult with whom you might, albeit briefly, experience familiar remnants of yourself. I began to rely on my mom friends in ways that surprised me, feeling them to be as essential to have around as Children's Motrin or liniment ointment for diaper rashes.

One of the moms in the group was a bawdy but fun Australian woman, who constantly told us all that we were "still hot" even with our "sagging tits." She deemed us "Yummy Mummies," a term I could never quite embrace, largely because I resented the implication that, in becoming a "mummy," one automatically relinquished one's "yummy-ness." Also, I didn't like being regarded as something akin to dessert. But I was there to fit in, not to quibble or rabble-rouse, so whenever the Bawdy Aussie insisted on beginning our dinners by bellowing a toast—"Here's to the yummiest mummies in New York City! We're still hot as fuck, ladies, amiright?"—I kept my trap shut, raised and then clinked my glass as enthusiastically as everyone else.

On this particular night, everyone was sloshed, chiming in with stories of shower sex and "babymoons" and weekends in swank hotels with children left home with nannies. I stayed uncharacteristically mum, knocking back what I recall to be quite a few dirty martinis. Noticing my silence after a few moments, the Bawdy Aussie lasered in on me: "Wot about you guys, Nancy?" she slurred.

"What about us . . . what?" I asked.

"Yeah," another of the moms said. "How the fuck do you guys . . ."

"Fuck . . . ?" supplied the Bawdy Aussie, to shrieks of laughter from the other Yummy Mummies. "Cos you guys . . . don't you all sleep in the same room? Bloody difficult then, in'it?"

There was a long pause, during which everyone tried to picture how Sam and I fucked.

"Ah don't moind telling ya," the Bawdy Aussie snickered, leaning in. "Yer a bit of a *guhl* crush f'me—know wot ah mean? Imagine you to be a pretty *lusty bird* when push comes to shove . . ."

The Bawdy Aussie, peering at me down her long nose, her mouth curled up in a lascivious grin, proceeded to scoop up and then lick the remnants of the praline profiteroles we'd ordered for the table off her finger. I couldn't help but feel I was next.

"Wot's yer secret?" she continued. "How. Do. You. Two. *Screw?*"

The question, spinning like a piñata, had my brain swinging left, right, up, and down in an effort to make contact so that a story—any story—could spill out. Finally, I came out with something both vague and suggestive:

"Well, there's always the sofa . . ."

What?

"*Oooooohhhhhhhhh!*" moaned all the moms in unison before continuing to lap up both the spirits and my perhaps not bold-faced but still stock lie. I remembered leaving the restaurant that night and insisting that I was going to walk the twenty blocks home instead of sharing a taxi with one of the other moms, only to hop right into a cab the minute the coast was clear and they were out of sight. I felt too stupid and ashamed to spend one more minute in their company. Speeding through the near-empty city, avenues whizzing by, I spent the ride rationalizing: *Well, at least I didn't gild the lily. It's not like I went down the road of "Oh, well, Sam and I, the minute the Bear is down for the night, screw to our hearts' content on the sofa, and we do this night after night after night, and it's fucking sublime."*

I had simply said, "There's always the sofa."

And there *was*. There was *always* a sofa.

It was not a sofa we did anything even remotely sexual on. But there was now—and there would always be—a sofa. But even if the evening's insinuated premise was sheer fantasy and the sofa in question was nothing more than a drab piece of furniture, taunting us with the suggestion of desires deferred, I found myself, as I sat on it thinking about my fib, our things, this life, haunted by the question, Could that change? And if so, what would it take? Often, when Sam had complained about our lack in the sack, I had countered with my yen to move into a place with two bedrooms instead of a single we all shared. While I had assumed (and internalized) the responsibility for our dearth, I had always maintained that at least some part of the reason we had no sex life was the lack of privacy. I had been approaching it all from the position that the only solution was to move, something Sam repeatedly pointed out we could not afford. But what if I operated from the premise that we needn't move in order to create the life I envisioned for us? What if we had everything we needed right here, right now, with maybe a little *jujhing*? What would it take to make my lie the truth?

When we began to renovate our house in LA, I'd found a housepainter heavily into feng shui. As we went through the place, deciding on colors, I at one point opened the den closet to show him where the previous owner's child had scribbled with crayon.

"I know it sounds petty," I told him, "because who'd know or see this but me, but . . . would you mind painting over this?"

He nodded knowingly and, without missing a beat, made a note on his pad: *Remove child chi.*

I became once again possessed with the idea of changing the chi in our home, only this time with the hope that it might re-create our dynamic. Perhaps it was a case of "putting the cart before the whore," but I had been waiting passively for the feelings to be stirred within, and in their absence, I thought, why not create the ideal conditions for them to be realized for only the cost of paint?

That evening, after I put the Bear to bed, I returned to the couch and sat there until Sam came home.

"What are you doing?" he said, putting his keys on the table.

"Envisioning ways to transform the space," I said.

"OK," he said. "Which space?"

"Everything."

"So . . . living room, bedroom . . ."

"The one that exists between us."

I looked at him. He nodded. This, unlike our boxes in storage, did not need unpacking.

"Where do we even start?" he asked.

"Paint," I said. "We start with paint."

So we picked some colors and painted. We rearranged. We *jujhed*. I went to our storage space and pulled out that leopard-print slipcover. I actually hugged it when I saw it again after all that time, and said aloud, not to a person but to fabric, "I've missed you."

I was so done being neutral.

We gave the Bear the entire bedroom and, using an old chinoiserie screen that had belonged to Sam's grandmother, created a boudoir for ourselves in the part of the living room that looked out into the courtyard below.

"It's not a living room anymore," I told Sam as we lay in bed alone for the first time in almost six years. "It's a loving room."

"I know you've been saying this," he said, turning to look around the living room, "but I'm just . . ."

He paused. He seemed overcome, unable to continue. But I wanted him to, needed him to.

"You're just what?" I prompted.

"I'm just . . . grateful," he said quietly. "Grateful to you for forcing us to create a real home, together."

I nodded and reached for his hand. I ignored the awkwardness of my reach, his acceptance of the gesture, and focused on how it felt for our fingers to be entangled. My mode, after all, had me believing that we not only had a new lease on our apartment, we had a new lease on life. So in spite of whatever niggling or unease there might have been, I was adhering instead to the memory of when it was as natural as breathing that I might reach for his hand, or he might reach for mine, when holding hands was something we did more than we didn't. But reality is an uninvited guest that has a way of intruding and staying put whether you want it to or not. Perhaps it doesn't occur in a single, definitive moment, a sneak attack on the senses. Sometimes, there comes a series of moments—some deeply troubling, some more innocuous— that bubble up over time. Like leftovers nuked in a microwave, these moments, because they are cooked from within, are often unassuming, leaving us unprepared for how much they can burn.

$\sim$

Just before New Year's, my friend Billy and I went to an old Village haunt called Cafe Bartok to listen to Sam perform a set of his original songs. When we arrived, a female acoustic guitar duo was still on. We found seats at a long communal table in the center of the room, then ordered drinks and listened to the duo Jewel-yodel their way through tunes about eating disorders and unrequited romance. When they finished, they passed the hat to me and Billy and their ten or so hipster friends before donning aprons to begin their shift bussing tables. The hipsters cleared out, and Sam's audience—including three lawyers from his old midtown law firm, the lawyer hubby of one of the Yummy Mummies, and a woman who'd at one time been married to Sam's uncle—settled into seats around us. Without much fanfare, Sam slid behind the piano, adjusted the mic, and for the next fifty minutes, complained about me in song. In fairness, there were a few in which the grousing was not about me directly, like the one about the subprime mortgage we had on our house in LA, or the one about this chick who'd never repaid the $500 Sam had loaned her in the midnineties. When Sam had told me about how excited he was for me to hear the "love songs" he'd written for me, I was genuinely looking forward to hearing them. I wasn't exactly picturing "Maybe I'm Amazed" or "Wonderful Tonight," but, hey, he was a good songwriter. I figured that the combo of our thorny history and his introspective nature might yield something along the lines of "Shit's Been Tough, but Dammit, I Fuckin' Love You, Girl" or even the poignant shade of a "You Don't Bring Me Flowers." But this wasn't that. This was, for the most part, song after song about being trapped by and ambivalent about a woman who was just terrible.

Afterward, Sam went to have drinks with his friends, and I went home to relieve the Bear's sitter. Billy and I walked in silence the twenty or so blocks to Chelsea, and when we arrived at my building, we stood on the street for a few moments. Though it was unseasonably warm for late December, I was nonetheless in my own private Antarctica, frozen in abject mortification.

"Well," Billy said, "on the plus side, you didn't throw anything into the hat."

"Oh, I did," I said. "The last shred of my dignity . . ."

Upstairs, I checked on the Bear, fast asleep in the bedroom, then tiptoed into the walk-in closet to disrobe for the evening. After a half-hearted attempt to put away my clothes, I sank nude to the floor, flinging strands of undercooked remedies and solutions toward the wall of my psyche, hoping something would stick. Even in the dark, I was beginning to see that no matter how hard we tried to get past the stuff that plagued us, our resentments, like unplucked weeds, had multiplied, becoming so unwieldy that eventually they had dwarfed anything good and healthy that might have grown. I might have known that things were not getting better, that for every positive step forward we were ultimately being rerouted back to the starting point by our unresolved feelings. But what I could not possibly have gleaned then, sitting bare-assed on the closet floor, was that we had long before hit dangerous levels of disenchantment, from which it would be impossible to return. The only two things of which I was certain were that the best of my husband's "love songs" was a paean to a mortgage broker in Van Nuys and that I would never again step foot in Cafe Bartok.

The creak of the closet door opening made me turn, expecting to see Sam, to hear him perhaps lamely apologize, saving me from my dread and telling me all the things I so badly wanted to hear. But in the same nanosecond that I heard the creak, I heard, too, the jinglejangle of tags, paws clacking against the concrete, nose sniffing out my exact locale. I was, as it so happened, on the receiving end of a rescue mission—one that made much more sense, and not just because, to my rescuer, the salty tears stinging my cheeks were an unadulterated delicacy. Sam's arrival home that night would be in silence, going by totally unnoticed. I would later discover him snoring on the leopard sofa, where he would sleep fully clothed, not just that night but for many nights to follow, while I, on the opposite side, in our newly fashioned boudoir, would sleep alone.

From this night forth, there would be a multitude of petty arguments that masked much deeper grievances, and roiling hostility would characterize our every encounter. The leopard sofa, where we never made love, would be where Sam continued to spend his nights, until one day, at winter's end, when a sublet in a building not too far from the wine shop would become available. We would not have a big discussion about what this bit of kismet signified; it would be remarkably calm and rational. "These digs are temporary" was what we would say to each other about the six-week interim crash pad meant to give us space to dial down the heat of our conflicts. "It's only six weeks," we would say.

Only weeks before fate presented us with that sublet, on the day I went to our storage unit to pull out the leopard-print slipcover, I found in the same box a yellow legal pad wedged in between the fabric. The pad contained notes and stray thoughts, all in Sam's handwriting, having to do with the pros and cons of keeping the puppy we'd bought so impetuously one Saturday afternoon at the mall. There was this idea that perhaps we were not going to be able to keep our precious Ira after all: our intractable Orthodox landlord had us scared shitless, I was having trouble finding dog-friendly buildings on such short notice, and Sam was having second thoughts about the whimsical way in which we came to own him in the first place. There were several pages of names and numbers—the doggy day care info, the contact information for the obedience trainer with whom I would have only one session.

"Never chase a dog—it's dangerous," she'd admonished. "If he gets loose, and you want him to come after you, run like hell in the other direction."

There were all kinds of beagle rescues and names of people and families who might be willing to take Ira in. I had at the time imagined these families as being typical all-American California types—blond, blue-eyed, athletic—the descendants of Steinbeck-like characters who had made their way west during the Depression. They'd be more obvious "beagle people" than Sam or me, people who surfed and played volleyball and barbecued and picnicked at the beach. The children would use words like *rad* unironically; the mom would be very tan and would wear no makeup save for very bright pink lipstick. These would not be people who would ever buy Ira a doggy massage or a high-heel-shaped dog toy called a "Jimmy Chew." They'd never have arguments that would make him shake, nor would they burden him by confiding their fears. These people would be light, unflappable, and fun—never fretful, never therapized, because they would always be "fine." The name *Ira* would confound them, so they would immediately dispense with it, renaming him *Buddy* or *Buster*. I was tormented not just by these visions or the growing sense that Sam was leaning toward giving Ira away, but more by my belief that it was possible, likely even, that my puppy would be happier with the blond Californians than he could ever be with me.

To further torture myself, I would lie in bed at night, with baby Ira splayed out across my boobs, playing out in my mind the scene of handing him over to this storybook family, imagining myself akin to Meryl Streep in *Sophie's Choice*, and Ira as her terrified daughter: "Take my dog, take my dog, take my dog!" I'd pretend-plead to the Californians. And though these frenzied imaginings occurred not in a war-torn country but rather in the luxury of a goose-down, duvet-covered California king, I was further plagued by what I recognized as the unabashed uncertainty of grief. "To love," Stephen the Buddhist therapist would many years later frequently intone, "is to become aware of loss with further losses to come. This is why love makes us so anxious even when it is good."

If there really was a choice, it was whether to experience pain in the now—horrible, but with less invested—or later, when, past the point of no return, it would be nothing short of horrendous.

But in truth, I didn't have a choice. The process of falling in love had already begun long before I played out my Streep scenarios, after which we would fall asleep, Ira still straddling my chest. There is something about two unconscious minds dancing a pas de deux in the shared dream space that forges a closeness that is as ineffable as it is unbreakable. It is what happens when we realize, finally, we are besotted, we are hooked, we are irrevocably done.

I still couldn't be totally sure, as I stood that day, examining a forgotten legal pad in storage, that I had not done Ira a disservice with my emotionally charged, thoroughly selfish insistence that we keep him. Like the day in July when I was unable to have Jim put him to sleep, I simply could not let him go, and as winter drew to a close, I was equally unwilling to relinquish anything—my dog, my husband, our family, my dreams. I could not see the value of "running like hell in the other direction." Instead, ignoring the imminent danger, I perpetuated the chase.

MARCH

Six

We Have No Secrets

I can't explain why, but not sharing a bed with my husband had the paradoxical effect of turning me, albeit briefly, into a domestic goddess. Perhaps it was something about the new terrain we found ourselves traipsing, but not long after Sam decamped to the six-week sublet, I became possessed with the idea of hosting an Easter dinner. Out of nowhere and without any warning, I wanted wholesome family traditions, and I wanted them yesterday. Forget that we'd never even celebrated Easter before or that for all intents and purposes we were Jewish—Easter, it suddenly occurred to me, was *everything*.

There was, after all, so much to love. *How,* I asked myself, *have I never realized how much I love Easter?* I mean, I loved the jelly beans and the fake grass; I loved Peter Cottontail (who either was or wasn't the Easter Bunny, I was never quite sure); I loved those decadent Cadbury Crème Eggs with the gooey, faux-raw-egg innards that looked perfectly vile but were, in fact, delicious. I loved that so many of the items needed to assemble a proper Easter basket could be found at Rite Aid. I loved that the grimy snow that rimmed the city was at last melting into the sewers, and soon there would be daffodils and birds and perhaps even a leaf or two. Easter, it seemed perfectly obvious to me, was like

Christmas only better, and now that I'd Rip-van-Winkled myself awake to all that I'd theretofore been missing, I vowed to never overlook this magical festival ever again.

"Why are all the kitchen towels splotched with colors?" Sam asked in the early hours of Palm Sunday, when he arrived so we could pretend to our daughter that he hadn't been sleeping ten blocks away. "It looks like a rainbow sneezed."

I explained my newfangled desire to host an Easter dinner.

And to my surprise, Sam suggested that we cohost.

"I think it would be good for the Bear," he explained, "for us to do something like this together, even, you know, while we're . . . not."

Of course I said yes. We had circumvented telling the Bear about our hiatus by breezily explaining "Dad is working late" and having Sam show up each morning before she woke, have breakfast with her, and take her to school as usual. Hosting the Easter dinner would be in line with this gambit, but Sam and I had also been keeping our little pause button under wraps to friends and family, and the one wrinkle in my Easter fantasy had been how to explain his absence to the guests. Now the whole thing could remain sub-rosa until we worked through our shit, and not a soul would be the wiser.

We planned our little wingding for as many guests as our dining table could accommodate (eight), and later that day, I typed up the menu, then sent it off to him for his perusal:

> *Mediterranean meze of hummus, tzatziki, and taramosalata with flatbreads*
> *Lentil salad with olives, tomatoes, fresh herbs, and feta*
> *Herb-crusted roast leg of lamb with baby fingerling potatoes*
> *Asparagus with lemon butter*

Fondant au chocolat with mint gelato
Cookies
Cheese

Then, two days later, Sam called me in the middle of the day.

"I have some bad news."

"Is it about Easter?" I asked.

"No," he said. "It's about Ciruela. We're closing."

"Closing?"

"Yes."

"Why?"

"Because we're hemorrhaging money," he said quietly.

"I mean, I know things have been slow, but . . . when?"

"Sunday."

Sunday? I screamed in my head (or what I *thought* was in my head; apparently, I was actually screaming out loud). Sunday was in only five days. Sunday was Easter. Yes, we had an evil landlord and a heinous tax increase and an owner whose heart was, well, elsewhere, but . . . *Oh my god, Sunday?*

"Yes, Sunday!" he screamed back. "I've been warning you about this for months—what part of 'we're in trouble' did you not understand?"

"Well, there's trouble and then there's *trouble*," I said, because what one does, when trying with all one's might to not stab out one's own eyes with the nearest sharp object or leap through the phone to enact similar violence on one's significant other, is unpack the relative shit-storminess of nouns.

"Well," he said flatly. "This is the latter. Or," he said, thinking it over, "it *was*. Now it's not so much a thing in 'trouble' as it is a thing that *was* in trouble and is *now* being put out of its misery."

My "trouble" in that moment, and in those that followed, was trying to keep straight in my head to which troubled thing Sam was referring. Given the current conditions, it could have applied to so very many.

I spent the next few days startled by how sad I felt by this news, by how much this eight-hundred-square-foot pain in the ass had meant to me now that it was gone. These feelings continued unabated until Easter Sunday. While some part of me spent the day preparing the Easter feast we'd decided to carry on with, maneuvering ingredients, utensils, and *mise-en-place* bowls across my kitchen's narrow countertop, the rest of me blinked about like Tinker Bell, frantically trying to call attention to the five years of evenings spent in the company of friends and strangers in an equally miniscule space I had initially loathed.

How can it be, I wondered, *that something I thought would be the bane of my existence gave me, in the end, a way of life? And that in doing so, it taught me that things, situations, and people can be both a conundrum and a gift.*

Standing there, preparing an absurdly grand meal for a holiday I had never been interested in until only the week before, I memory-skipped through the dinners, parties, art events, business meetings, birthdays, memorials, bitch sessions, and bar-hangs that made Ciruela—albeit fleetingly—the ne plus ultra in affordably groovy Village haunts, and me its eternally proud doyenne.

Billy will come by to help make the lamb; the guests will arrive; Sam and I will avoid eye contact. We will do this when people compliment the food; we will do this during toasts to the perished Ciruela; we will do this even when the Bear asks us all to join hands and take turns saying what we wanted to "say goodbye to" and what we wanted "to grow." Though I will not recall any of our answers to the Bear's query, or, for that matter, much else about the evening, I will remember, with great clarity, this moment of joining hands and feeling somewhat subdued by the question. In time, a few other moments will glisten through the cracks whenever I think back on my one paschal repast: the terrifically hostile post-din-din cha-cha Sam and I danced to Dean Martin's "Ain't

That a Kick in the Head"; the special Easter egg hostess gift my friend Charity brought me, its entrails blown out through a tiny hole and its remaining shell Sharpied with the colorful Ciruela logo; Ira sleeping on top of my feet, under the table, as we dined.

It was a weird ending to a weird week, which begot another one in which things only got weirder: the day after Easter, I would wake up to find Ira back in his spot in the bedroom closet for the first time since that fateful day the previous July. I knew this could mean only one thing, and as soon as the Bear was off to school, I gathered Ira up in a blanket and racewalked over to Chelsea Animal Hospital. Ira's disease, which had granted a relatively calm nine-month cease-fire, was now gunning for us like an armored tank.

"He's badly anemic," Jim said, looking at the blood work numbers.

"How badly?" I asked. "Badly, meaning it's . . . over?"

Jim shook his head.

"No. I think there's stuff we can do, but it's expensive."

My heart sank. The last thing I wanted was to have to throw in the towel because I couldn't afford treatment.

"Like what?" I asked. "What are the things we could do?"

"Well," Jim sighed, "there's Epogen, which is a drug given by injection to stimulate the bone marrow into producing red blood cells. And I would also say that he needs a series of blood transfusions, and we'd give him some iron supplements, too."

"And if he had these things?" I asked.

"If he had these things, he'd feel better."

"So, I mean, money aside, doing these treatments wouldn't be a crazy thing to do?"

"No, not a crazy thing to do at all."

I stood frozen for a moment, rubbing Ira's ears between my fingers like a security blanket. *I can't afford this,* I thought to myself. *I really*

*can't . . . but then again, how can I afford not to try, especially if it would
make him feel better—and who knows, maybe even revivify him like
treatment did back in July?*

"If he was your dog—" I started to say.

"I'd do it," Jim said, "yes."

*If only I had a million dollars. If only I had pet insurance. If only I'd
been better at science and become a vet.*

"There's also another wrinkle," Jim said.

"What's that?"

"Well, like I said, it ain't cheap, and the other thing is that eventually
the Epogen will stop working, because his immune system will develop
antibodies that cause it to be rejected. And I don't have any way of
knowing when that would be, you know?"

I nodded. I did know. But knowing that the future was uncertain
and without guarantee was a way of living to which I had grown
very accustomed. And despite having just celebrated the holiday of
"resurrection," death, it seemed, hovered all around us. I wanted to
make this all go away. And barring that, I wanted to at the very least
make this go away *for today*. So I walked to the front desk, slapped
$1,500 of injections, transfusions, and medications on my American
Express card, and told myself I'd think about how to get the money to
pay it off later. It was all very Scarlett O'Hara: Atlanta was burning,
Ashley was marrying Melanie, Tara was screwed. But come hell or high
water, I'd figure out a way. A "way," by the way, that did not include
telling Sam—about the treatments or, more importantly, the money.
This was to be a cooling period, so why raise the heat? *I'm not* not *telling
him,* I reasoned to myself. *I'm just not telling him* this minute, *because
by the time I'll need to apprise him, the whole thing will be paid off. There
will come a day, when we are significantly past this time of strife, when I
will tell Sam all kinds of truths about what was going on with me during
this interlude. But for now,* I thought, *I want to have one fewer bell to
answer, one fewer egg to fry.*

Within hours of the transfusion, Ira is, once again, his old self—playful, eating, tail wagging—and no matter how concerned I am about being in the hole for the cash, I do not, for one second, rue my decision.

~

The following afternoon, I had lunch with my old friends Theresa and Mark to brainstorm ways to pay off my Amex. Theresa, a no-nonsense girl from Queens, and Mark, a former music executive, were both endless fonts of information, especially when it came to how to make a quick buck. The consensus was that my best bet would be to sell my jewelry—all of it (or as much of it as I was willing to part with). I had some things left to me by my grandmother. I had no idea what they were worth—if anything at all—but I'd always thought they might come in handy on a rainy day. Given the deluge, it seemed that day had arrived.

A few days later, Theresa will take me, along with my small bag of trinkets, to "the Garage," a flea market on Twenty-Fifth Street, to see what, if anything, I might be able to sell. There, Theresa will introduce me to Wanda, a broad so scary it is not a stretch to imagine her doing time with Aileen Wuornos. Wanda will then introduce me to a jittery low-level mobster named Mickey.

Mickey is missing teeth; Wanda is missing a conscience.

Gold is at "an all-time high"; I am at an all-time low.

The confluence of these things can mean only one thing: kismet.

Wanda will pick through my bag, eyes darting, never settling for too long on the piece she is ostensibly examining through her loupe. She seems blasé, more so when a piece is of value. It is a technique employed to lowball you out of your bauble for a song. It almost always works.

"How much you want for the ring?" she will ask me, momentarily ignoring the items in the bag to fix her gaze instead on the engagement ring I am suddenly wearing after years of not, to insist to myself and to the world that, yes, that's right, I am still *married*.

Though slight in size, the rose-cut stone and Edwardian-era setting give it great appeal. They don't make rings like this anymore. Wanda knows this. She also knows my husband and I are having a "break" and that I am hard up for cash.

"Actually," I say, demurring, "I'm not ready to part with it."

Wanda smiles, then makes a great show of pretending to see someone in the distance behind me. She is a bad actress, obvious and try-too-hard-y, milking her act to embarrassing excess, squinting her eyes and scrunching up her nose to feign bemusement, then widening her eyes in recognition, then squinting and scrunching in bemusement once again at this phantom person. *It shouldn't matter,* I will think to myself as I watch her lurid pantomime, *but when reduced to hocking heirlooms to score drugs for your dying dog, it would be nice if the person ripping you off could be the Meryl Streep of swindlers.*

Wanda will tell me my best bet is to sell the majority of my things to a refiner.

"Sometimes you just gotta know when to scrap it," she will say, invoking what is to become a catchphrase Theresa and I will repeat ad nauseam. We will use this mantra in the years to come about personal items, remainders, relationships. "Scrapping it" will never come easily to me, whether I know its time has come or not. But I will know—in that way one knows one is in the midst of a pivotal moment—that as soon as they pass Wanda's crooked lips, these are words I will never forget.

Reluctantly, because they are competitors, Wanda will call for Mickey, who will ascend from his booth located on the more subterranean level of the Garage, because it is Mickey, and not Wanda, who has the direct line to "the scrapper." And though Wanda will buy a few pieces of my jewelry, it will be Mickey who will fork over the lion's share of the cash I walk away with that day, spiriting my grandma's gold cigarette cases and broken bracelets away to be melted down by the Hasids on Forty-Seventh Street. I will be undecided as to which feels more profoundly empty—my bag or my heart—as I walk west on Twenty-Fifth Street toward home, but I know for sure that, should the day ever come when I have to sell my engagement ring, I will never—no matter how broke or desperate I am—sell it to Wanda or Mickey.

There is something else I will sell to pay off vet bills: an Elsa Peretti necklace from Tiffany—a gift from Sam for my fortieth birthday—that Mark will list for me on eBay.

"Anything Tiffany holds its value," he'd told me the day we'd had lunch with Theresa. "You won't get exactly what you paid for it, but close . . ."

The necklace—a single diamond in a bezel on a slender gold chain—is, aside from my wedding and engagement rings, my favorite piece of jewelry. I love how it looks, this tiny droplet of light resting in the notch of my throat: understated, a tad erotic, and chic. Wearing it makes me feel like some glam seventies icon who has Halston on speed dial. Mostly, though, I love that it came from Sam, who bought it for me just after we went through what had been, till that point, the most trying time of our marriage. Since that moment, for just about six years, the necklace has been a symbol to me of how, no matter what, Sam still *sees me* and loves me more than anyone. I know it is just a "thing," but it is a thing that means so many other things—about our love and what we've gone through together—and I hate having to say goodbye to it.

"Are you sitting down?" Mark will ask about a week after he lists the necklace. "Carly Simon bought your necklace."

Carly Simon. Bought. *What?*

Mark will go on to explain that he received a few questions about the necklace, its size, and its provenance—that the person doing the querying had shared that their daughter had lost an almost identical Elsa Peretti necklace, which the buyer wanted to replace. A brief negotiation on price will ensue, after which the buyer will transfer funds into Mark's PayPal account and give him a name and shipping address. The funds will come from a "Carly Simon"; the item is to be shipped to the same, with a residential address in Martha's Vineyard. There is not even the pretense of ambiguity, no business manager or assistant to separate or shield the celebrity from the Great eBay Unwashed. It is so refreshingly forthright.

The Carly Simon story might have been good enough on its own merit, but I will need it to mean more than just another anecdote on the randomness of life and celebrities who dig luxury items on sale. I will need to believe that Carly Simon's daughter losing the same necklace I needed to unload—two seemingly random albeit simultaneous events— was in fact a predetermined and inevitable bit of Jungian synchronicity. That somehow, Carly Simon, the archetype of soft-rock, feministic insouciance, extrasensorially perceived that *I* hadn't "got time for the pain," and, like the best imaginary girlfriend ever, coughed up almost the exact amount I charged to the American Express card I should surely have left home without. And the more I parse this divinely inspired, psychic parallel, the more convinced I will be, because there is actually a bit more to my crazy Carly connection:

Twenty-one years earlier, in what felt like another life entirely, I had met Carly Simon, on Valentine's Day, 1990, through my then boyfriend, a jazz bassist who played with Harry Connick Jr. The Bass Player and Harry were hired to play a few tunes with Carly on her HBO special, in support of her album *My Romance*. Harry had ushered in a new dawn of ersatz Sinatra-type crooners, and every pop star, it seemed, was swan-diving into the fray with a "standards album." Carly, plagued for years with debilitating panic attacks, could sing in front of people only if (a) she basically knew everyone in the audience, (b) it was taped so there was no fear of fuckups, and (c) she was hopped up on beta-blockers.

The concert special was comprised of the standards Carly did on her album, save for one glorious moment when, accompanied by my boyfriend and Harry, she sang a bossa nova version of her 1973 hit "We Have No Secrets." The final track on side one of Carly's seminal 1972 album of the same name, "We Have No Secrets," is about how Carly and James Taylor were super groovy and told each other about the people they'd banged before (and during?) their love affair—because there's no worse affront to a "Me Decade" couple than "having secrets," except of course how totally shitty having the knowledge ultimately makes you feel.

In my quixotic youth, I, too, fancied myself the type of chick who could be "cool" with full disclosures and free love. In fact, when I first started seeing the Bass Player, I told him that I eschewed the more conventional strings of attachment most women expected; I was "fine" with "whatever." I didn't "need no piece of paper from the city hall." I even told him that if he ever happened to be playing a gig at a jazz club in my neighborhood and felt like making love, no matter the time of night, he should give me a call—because I was "cool." And though I meant it when I said it, I was unprepared for how taxing being "cool" could be on my psyche, because once the Bass Player took me up on my sex offer, I was in love with him by the time it was over, and never wanted him to leave. This of course put a damper on my declarations of no strings, to say nothing of my nascent "coolness." And though the Bass Player and I entered into an exclusive relationship, his penis apparently never received the memo, remaining a Lothario with every groupie from here to Merzouga. And each time he pleaded with me to disregard his indiscretions, claiming that he'd never have sex with a road bimbo again, I'd believe it (or want to)—until one day, my "cool" having long since evaporated, I became the scorned harpy I had sworn

I could never in a million years become, and we finally broke up for good. It was awful and devastating, and I thought I'd never recover, and then I did, and then, lemons to lemonade, the whole incident became the fodder that begot my writing career.

But back to Carly Simon: I could not have been more delighted when the Bass Player told me of the gig and that he'd be accompanying Carly on a few tunes. I was even more ecstatic when he asked me to attend the filming, where I'd be sitting ringside. Along with most women of my generation, I had been a Carly fan forever. Like songs by Carole and Joni (and later Stevie and Rickie Lee), Carly's tunes, ever present on the muffled radio of my mother's faux-wood-paneled station wagon, peppered the emotional soundtrack of my childhood. I hung on her every sensually plaintive, memoir-infused word as if it were scripture, as if she were singing only to me. What it meant, exactly, to have "clouds in [her] coffee" may have eluded me, but I understood that, whatever was going on, Carly would eventually figure it out and, by extension, so would I.

The night before the Bass Player went off to his first rehearsal with Carly, we went out to dinner at our favorite Indian food joint, Mitali West, and just for kicks, over our chicken murgh tikka, I started to sing "You're So Vain."

"Well, I hear you went to Sara-to-ga / And your horse, naturally, won / Then you flew your Learjet up to Nova Sco-tia / To see the tot-al e-clipse of the sun—"

The Bass Player stopped me.

"That's not how it goes, baby," he said. "There weren't no Learjets in '71 or whenever that song came out . . ."

"What are you talking about?" I laughed. "Of course that's the lyric!"

"Nah—come on . . . ," he said, waving me off.

"So what's she saying, then?" I demanded.

The Bass Player thought for a second, then began to sing:

"Well, I hear you went up to Sara-to-ga / And your horse, naturally, won / Then you flew your *li'l* jet up to Nova Sco-tia / To see the tot-al e-clipse of the sun . . ."

I began to laugh hysterically—was he kidding?

"Li'l?!"

"Somethin' like that—"

"*Li'l* jet?"

"As in *little*, but, you know—"

"Li'l?"

"Yeah."

Totally incredulous, I burst out laughing again.

"Ask Carly tomorrow," I dared him. "I wanna hear what she says."

The minute the Bass Player arrived home from rehearsal the next night, I asked him, "Well? What did Carly have to say about the 'li'l jet'?"

"Carly says you were correct," the Bass Player told me sheepishly, pulling me to him for a kiss.

"Of course I was," I said, giggling. "What'd she say?"

"She said, 'Good thing you have a smart girlfriend.'"

The next night, we arrived at the theater, which had been done up to look like an old-school nightclub, with chairs around little round tables tricked out in white linens and dimly lit table lamps.

Shortly before shooting began, the Bass Player introduced me to Carly.

"So, you're the one who knows about Learjets, huh?" she asked me, smiling that wide, toothy, totally magnificent Carly Simon smile.

I couldn't believe it.

I also couldn't believe it when I got to sit a little over a foot away from her—the one and only Carly Simon, bedecked in a series of glamorous frocks, elbow-length gloves, and dazzling bijous—as she sang love song after love song after love song. Just like in my mother's station wagon all those years before, I felt as if she were singing just to me.

At one point, in between takes, she was even *talking* just to me, candidly kibitzing about the marvels of benzodiazepines. "Isn't it amazing the things you can do on Valium?" she asked, smiling slyly, while grips and other technicians swarmed about, repositioning cameras: worker bees with their queen. I laughed and nodded, not because I knew much about what she was talking about, but because I wanted to talk to her more, my new bestie, Ms. Carly Simon. But before I could ask her some sort of follow-up, like whether she preferred Valium to Xanax, her newish hubby bounded up to her side for some quick sugar, whispering into her bejeweled ear and stroking her luscious golden mane. I remember thinking, as I watched them, how happy I was for her that she had found this handsome, terribly affectionate man, following her bruising breakup with the philandering junkie the world knew as "Sweet Baby James," and what it all said about the heart's ability to regenerate.

A few days after Mark sends off my necklace in its Tiffany Blue Box to Carly in Martha's Vineyard, I dig out the VHS tape I saved of the Carly Simon HBO concert special and lie back on the leopard couch, with Ira stretched out alongside me, to watch it for the first time since it was originally televised. There is an excessively dewy quality to it all stylistically, but Carly, at forty-five, the same age I am as I lie there, is even more enchanting than I recall.

I watch her; I watch me, watching her.

I am oddly devoid of the usual denigratory musings on my looks, feeling instead fond, protective even, of the girl at the front table, as if she were not me but an old pal I hadn't seen in a long time. As the credits role, Carly invites the audience to come up and dance. I watch myself—long, straight hair, full-on Jane Birkin–style bangs, vintage blue velvet pantsuit, arms draped around the broad shoulders of the Bass Player—in the lower right corner of the frame. I am reminded of how madly in love I was with the Bass Player; how innocent and wide-eyed I was; how naive, to the end, I would remain to his chronically wandering peen. But in early 1990, I was barely twenty-four years old and not yet able to admit to the limitations I shared with the Carly of "We Have No Secrets," whose attempts at rationalization were so at odds with how she felt inside.

Within a few months of that Valentine's Day, the Bass Player would come clean. I would learn all about the groupies I am blissfully unaware of as we sway to the orchestra playing what Carly described as "make-out music." Carly, dancing with Harry, has no clue that her lovey-dovey hubby will one day admit to being a closeted homosexual. For people with "no secrets," we seem to be lousy with them. And that will include Sam, who has a few of his own left to reveal.

Seven

Someone Left the Cake out in the Rain

It was spring. There had been terrible rains, threats of hurricanes, and even a tornado. But finally, and seemingly overnight, spring had sprung in New York, and everything was alive and blooming. The streets were flooded with color: daffodils, hipsters, babies, tulips, lovers, lilacs, and dogs of all shapes and sizes—happy, scampering, robust. Sunshine and life, everywhere I looked, unabashed and glorious. It was amid this spectacular landscape that I discovered Sam was having an affair.

We had just celebrated our twelfth wedding anniversary, and things had been improving since our "unofficial separation" had commenced several weeks before. Although Sam appeared at times remote and edgy, we were back in couples counseling, and there had been a distinct softening between us. It seemed that the "break" was giving us each time to reflect, so that together we could cultivate, in the words of our therapist, "a shared sense of each other's suffering." It wasn't perfect, but I still believed in the curative powers of love—just as the Tibetans believe in magical birds and the Catholics believe in Jennifer Jones and *The Song of Bernadette*.

We had met for dinner, on the eve of our anniversary, at a beautiful boîte in the deepest reaches of the West Village, the scene theretofore of so many happy occasions. When I arrived, Sam was already there, waiting for me at the table. We had a no-gifts edict, and so none were exchanged, but as I slid onto the banquette next to him, Sam handed me a card. While the waiter took our drink order, I read the following:

Happy anniversary, Nancy. We still have so much to celebrate. —S.

I don't know what it was about those two sentences that gave me pause. The sentiment was warm, and the words relatively innocuous, and yet a whisper of fear fluttered briefly in my stomach. As I read the card over and over, my eyes continually lingered on the word *still*. "We *still* have so much to celebrate." Still. Still . . . ?

I began to silently unpack this little word, as though it held the key to unlocking the mystery of our fate. Did it mean *still*, in spite of all that has gone down, all the shit that you've done or I've done, and the awful way we seem to make each other feel—*still*, despite all of that, we *still* might be able to . . . what? Tolerate more? Because we *still* have a history together, and even though it's a mostly rocky one, it *still* exists, and we *still* owe it to each other / our child / the institution of marriage itself to soldier on? Or was the *still* more positive, as in, we really do *still* have a future; there really is *still* hope; you are *still* my best friend; I *still* love you?

Perhaps it's heretical, but I always hated the Commodores' song "Still." I loathed the treacly lyrics and weirdly contrived pauses, and every time it came on the radio and I heard those opening piano chords, followed by Lionel Richie's ridiculously drawn-out "Laaaaa-daaaay," I wanted to throw up. The whole thing was so ponderous that whenever I was subjected to its mournful strains, I couldn't help but think, *Well, no wonder she "laughed at [you]" and then dumped you!*

I'm of the mind that there's nothing more delicious than a depressing breakup ballad mired in heartbreak and metaphor, but let's face it: "Still" is no "A Case of You." For that matter, it's also no

"Easy" (Like Sunday Morning). And yet there I was, listening to "Still" crescendo in the soundtrack of my mind and relishing every last note as though it were the be-all and end-all anthem of blessed devotion.

I remembered reading somewhere that Lionel Richie had written "Still" for some friends who had decided to end their marriage in order to save their friendship. The thing about Sam and me was that, from the moment we met, we had had this incredible bond. And no matter what had gone down, Sam was my best friend. And it was the diminishment of this connection—which had once been so easy, so kindred, so very, very real—that to me was the saddest and most distressing aspect of our marital discord.

For all the optimism I had been feeling in the days and weeks leading up to our anniversary, I was suddenly overcome with sadness as I considered the very real prospect of what we both stood to lose if it all didn't work out. If we were unable to save, in the words of Lionel Richie, "what we both had found," would we, like the couple for whom the song was written, find a way to stay together, at the very least, as friends who loved each other . . . *still?*

It was something I might have asked Sam as we sat in that wonderful restaurant, surrounded by stunning floral displays, beneath one of Julian Schnabel's glorious broken-plates paintings, had I not been so afraid of the answer. Instead, slipping the card back into the torn envelope, I held my glass of Grüner Veltliner aloft and asked the only question I could possibly muster without bursting into tears: "To us?"

Sam, raising his glass, concurred with the quietest, most restrained clink I'd ever heard. "To us . . ."

~

There had been another reason to raise a glass that night: my new job writing for David Letterman's bandleader/sidekick, Paul Shaffer.

When he wasn't on *Late Show* duty, Paul Shaffer was doing his shtick on syndicated terrestrial radio with his own daily feature, *Paul Shaffer's Day in Rock*. I had been offered the job after being recommended by the previous writer, the husband of a friend, who had just landed a job in Los Angeles. It seemed promising: a comedy-writing gig, in which I would be the lone scribe. The job entailed research, pop-culture savvy, narrative and editorial skills, joke writing, and of course, cognizance of songs from the heyday of rock and roll. For each day, I would be required to write two stories, totaling sixty seconds, pertaining to that date in rock history; each "script" would contain two weeks' worth of stories. Twice a month, we would head into the old CBS Studios on Tenth Avenue, where, in a three-hour session, Paul would prerecord the stories that would air six weeks later.

It all happened very quickly: the friend's hubby called me, I told him I was interested, and later that afternoon I found myself in a nondescript midtown office, meeting with the producer of Paul's feature, a towering Jew-jock named Rob with the countenance of a good-natured frat boy. We shook hands, and before I even got my ass in the seat in front of his desk, Rob cut right to the chase.

"Can you write like a man?"

There it was, the turd in the punch bowl. It can be awfully tempting, for those of us who are vaginally inclined, to seize a moment like this as an opportunity to reflect on a lifetime of feeling unfairly dismissed due to our genitalia. As much as I aspire to do so, I have never been able to summon the righteous fury of my more spirited Right-On Sisters. In these instances, I become uncharacteristically quiet, and my thoughts empirical—like a latter-day Margaret Mead observing a primitive society eating with their feet, or pissing triumphantly on poison berries. I won't lie: I enjoy judging the perpetrator of overt sexism as much as the next gal, but I have found over the years that it is much more gratifying to revel in the strange sort of relief such moments provide.

Because, if nothing else, there is a quiet comfort in knowing that, no, you have not misunderstood.

"Depends on the man," I replied coolly. "Are we talking about an actually *funny* man?"

"Look—no offense," Rob said, backpedaling just a tad. "It's just that Paul is, you know . . . he's *old-school*. He needs to feel confident that whoever's got the gig is going to be able to write for him in his particular voice—"

"A reasonable request . . ."

"And, well . . ." Rob paused, leaned in a bit, and even though the nearest person was out his office door and at least ten cubicles away, murmured sotto voce, "He likes to get a little, you know . . . *loose* in the studio . . ."

"Loose?"

"Yeah, you know . . . *raunchy* . . ."

While this tidbit conjured images of a partially clothed, spliff-toking Paul, swinging gaily from a chandelier as debauched naked women lay shackled to recording studio equipment, I remained as placid as a Zen master.

"OK . . ."

"He likes to talk about *hot chicks* and *big tits* and, you know, who's got a *great ass*, yadda yadda, and . . . you know . . . ?"

Sure, I knew. I had worked with big-name male comedians of the "women aren't funny" variety many times in the past, and this predilection for cataloguing female assets as a way of "blowing off steam" was as standard as they came. In those bygone days, I'd hoodwinked myself into believing that I gave *zero* fucks about it, rejecting any notion that I was in a hostile environment by focusing all my energy on one thing: *being funny*. Because as long as I was considered *funny*, something the men with whom I worked wholeheartedly believed to be impossible for anyone lacking a penis, I was doing a damn good job of masking my inferior sex; my position was safe, and I was "on my way."

Sitting there in Rob's office, I realized that I had come a long way from the days when I was willing to swallow my feelings or dismiss power trips or even rudeness, and the thought of having to bide my time while the men I worked for verbally jacked off left me cold. But the fact of the matter was this: I needed the job. And necessity is the mother of convention. The pay wasn't great (in fact, it was pretty appalling), but the experience would be invaluable if I wanted to get into this particular kind of comedy writing, and who knew, maybe I did. Plus, aside from the bimonthly recording sessions, I could work from home, which would enable me to take care of both my growing child and my ailing dog. I would learn the skill of joke writing—something I had never done before but nonetheless felt confident I would master, and once I did, I could move on to greener pastures with the blessings (and recommendations of) a comedy legend. I even imagined how impressed and happy my husband would be with me; how it might reinvigorate his enthusiasm, admiration, and love if I could show him how ballsy I was to score this cool gig on a dime, how inured I was willing to make myself to the soft sexism of the Boys' Club as a means to support my family and put dinner on the table every night. I was so tired of being the agent of Sam's distress, tired of being such a profound disappointment to virtually every man with whom I had been intimate. In fact, the only male who had not let it be known that I had failed him in some remarkable way was Ira, whose declining health was the only reminder I needed.

Anyway, somehow, this all motivated me, in this moment in time, to fight like hell: I wanted this shitty-paying-but-impressive-on-paper job, and I wanted it with every fiber of my being, as if landing it would bring about not just a reversal of fortune but my very salvation.

"Look," I told Rob, pressing on. "None of that's a problem for me; I won't be offended or call the cops or the press or human resources—"

"Well, see, the problem isn't *you*," Rob said, jumping in. "It's Paul. He needs to feel *comfortable* to, you know, talk shit the way he's used to. And generally when there's a chick around, well . . . it changes the *vibe*, you know? I just don't want him to lose his edge or feel like he has to be all polite just cuz you're there."

No. We wouldn't want that. I was admittedly stumped: What could I say to that? Either he would be comfortable or he wouldn't be, and there wasn't a damn thing I could do about it, aside from investing in a strap-on. There was a long pause.

"Well," Rob sighed. "We need a writer. And unless I can find someone else, I'd like you to audition. Can you get me five stories by tomorrow morning?"

I knew that whatever I did would not just have to be as good or even better than what a man would do, it would also have to prove that I was no wilting flower. It meant that I would have to come up with material as subversively blue as possible without crossing into gross indecency. So with that in mind, I went home and proceeded to write up five of the filthiest (true) stories I could find about the history of rock and roll. I read them over, made sure the language was as euphemistic as possible so that it would pass muster with FCC regulations, and immediately emailed them off to Rob. Ten minutes later, he called me.

"Where'd you find the story about Chuck Negron's cock breaking after fucking too many chicks?"

"It's in his memoir, *Three Dog Nightmare* . . ."

"His dick broke?" Rob was incredulous.

"He described it as, quote, 'bursting open like a hot dog in a microwave,' so . . . um . . . yeah . . ."

"OK." Rob paused. "Any ideas for a Three Dog Night song that could tie in?"

"How's 'Mama Told Me Not to Come'?"

After Rob finished laughing, he told me I was hired.

~

Shortly after midnight, about a week after our anniversary, I am propped up in bed with Ira asleep beside me, listening to the original version of the song "MacArthur Park." I am looking for potential fodder for a Shaffer script, and "MacArthur Park," with its fanfares, orchestral breaks, and florid imagery, seems ripe with comedic possibility. Unlike the Donna Summer disco version, the original, sung by the actor Richard Harris, is Shakespearean, psychedelic, and borderline campy, all of which is perfect for Paul. I begin to scan the lyrics, looking for a punch line:

> *MacArthur Park is melting in the dark*
> *All the sweet, green icing flowing down*
> *Someone left the cake out in the rain*
> *I don't think that I can take it*
> *'Cause it took so long to bake it*
> *And I'll never have that recipe again*

For years, I thought "MacArthur Park" was about a bunch of stoners who, escaping a torrential downpour, abandon their dessert. In fact, the song describes a painful breakup, one that—even with the purple prose and overwrought execution—strikes me now as not only not funny but also strangely poignant.

Just as I conclude that I might need to scrap the "MacArthur Park" story, I hear the ping of an incoming text message. It is a forwarded text from a number with a 305 area code that I don't recognize but that I nonetheless know is from Miami and has, for some reason, been forwarded from Sam's phone to mine:

Don't worry—I'll let you sleep tonight. ;) You come up for a steak and salad, and then zzzzz . . .

It takes me a minute, but once I grasp that what I am reading is a *sext* between Sam and some chick from Miami, my heart begins to pound and words bounce wildly off the inside of my skull: *Miami, steak, salad, fucking (wink!), steak, salad, fucking, Miami (wink!), Miami (wink!), Miami (wink, wink, wink!), zzzzzzzzzzzzzzzzzzzz* . . . Over and over and over, words swirling, heart racing, until, wending my way out of the K-hole and into mortified comprehension, I collapse onto the bed in hysterics. I don't know how long I lie there, weeping, reeling, before I hear the thwacking of the tail against the comforter, followed by the feel of a warm, rhythmic tongue bath. I peer through the veil of tears to see the droopy black lips, the twitching black nose, the whiskers swaying like dune grass on the road to the beach.

I turn over onto my stomach to face him, and I cry louder and he licks harder.

"What the *fuck* am I gonna do now, doggy?"

I search those doleful brown hound eyes, as I have a squillion times in the past, for answers, and never have they been less forthcoming than they are now. Resting his head on top of my hands, he sighs deeply and closes his eyes.

~

Two days later, Sam and I are sitting in our therapist Stephen's garretlike office. Sam, having been confronted with the infidelity and with my anguish over the manner in which it was discovered, is apologizing. He reiterates that, while the transgression itself was "a necessary part of [his] process," the text I received was inadvert. A cyber-snafu, a virtual fuckup.

"I never wanted to hurt you," he keeps saying. "That was never my intent."

I do not respond to this; I am too busy keening and rocking back and forth on Stephen's couch.

Stephen suggests that the ability to face a crisis and find a way to move on is what defines the beginning of true marriage. "If you choose to make your marriage work," he remarks, "there's no other arena I can think of that can create the same kind of growth."

"We're not ready to work on it," Sam counters. "We need—I need—space and time to explore."

I listen mutely as Stephen interrogates Sam:

"Are you willing to forgo continuing the affair for now?"

"No. But I have told her I am not ready to leave my marriage . . ."

"Do you want a divorce?"

"No—I don't want a divorce. We're not ready for that. We're not there yet. But something has changed in me, and I'm not sure anymore what I want. I need time."

"How much time?" I ask, finally having located my larynx.

"I don't know . . ."

"A month? Two months? Six months? When you say 'time,' what does this mean?"

"I don't know."

"You can't hope for renewal when you are creating intimacy with another," Stephen says, fingering the tiny om charm that dangles from his leather choker. "These two concepts are diametrically opposed."

There is a pause; Stephen switches his gaze between us, his ocher-rimmed orbs floating to and fro like Ping-Pong balls. Finally, leaning forward in his chair, he speaks, uninterrupted, for the next few minutes.

"Look—you two have been slaves to a pattern of despair for a long time. Duking it out, unable—quite simply—to get past the anger. But all the things required to make a relationship flourish—love, possibility, invitation, curiosity, concern for the 'we'—can only exist where there is no anger. Anger is just corrosive and leads only to more anger. And blame. And then more anger. And the only thing that melts anger is sorrow and grief.

"If the two of you could get to a place of mutual sorrow and grief, then perhaps genuine apology and forgiveness can be granted and a new love forged. You would have to declare your marriage dead: a first marriage to one another that is dead and gone and mourned, after which a new one could emerge. But this, of course, is only possible if both people are not just at a place of true grief and sorrow where they can get beyond the anger, but only if there is also a genuine desire to make such a new relationship happen with the other."

Sam is not sure he wants this; he repeats that he needs time.

"I want this," I say. "I am willing to work on this, but I don't see how I can if you continue seeing the chick from Miami. You can't have your cake and fuck it, too . . ."

"I am in a process," Sam says again. "I need time."

"Well, Nancy," Stephen says. "You don't have to put up with this. You don't have to agree to these terms. And if you said you can't do this, I wouldn't blame you—it's not fair. It's not right."

Sam begins to cry softly. "I never wanted to hurt you," he says. "I never wanted to hurt you . . ."

I look at him. I study his face the way I used to when we were first together and I'd watch him sleep. *Is she young?* I want to ask him about the chick from Miami. *Is she hot?* It dawns on me that these are the same questions my yoga friend had for me about our Brazilian babysitter—the one about whom I never suspected a thing, because Sam was not the kind of guy who strayed. *Was that stupid of me?* I want to ask Sam now. *Was it cavalier? Why didn't I know then, as I stood on that sweltering sidewalk, that my whole world could change, and that it would, and soon—like that very day?* "Are you interested in staying married?" my friend had laughingly chided. *I am,* I silently tell Sam. *But are you? Please tell me you are; please make this all go away . . .*

The buzzer rings, signaling that Stephen's next couple has arrived and our session has come to a close. On our way out the door, I turn back to Stephen: "What do we do now?"

"We proceed forward," he says gently.

But as Sam and I trudge down his rickety steps, I can't figure out how I can possibly proceed forward when all I want to do is stop time.

~

In the ensuing days, I find myself thoroughly disoriented, moving remarkably slowly—drifting, really, from one activity to the next. Every task is refracted through the acid trip of pain, the upheaval of infidelity. Like a dervish, I twist and turn and howl, blame flinging off with every whirl—toward Sam, then ricocheting back—until I am positive it is all my fault. My emotions synthesize into a blend of blind rage, crippling fear, and frantic crystal gazing.

Late one morning, I am cleaning the bathroom cabinet and find a bar of soap. It is just a regular bar of Ivory soap: bland, boring, and otherwise unremarkable. It has been sitting there, probably since the day it was bought, its position as the "next soap bar to be used" usurped heedlessly by another bar and another bar and another, until, over time, because it remained unseen, cloaked under the morass of other, more prominent toiletries, it was ignored, forgotten about—until now. Its wrapping has taken on the sheen of defeat; it is no longer gleaming white but, instead, a sort of dank yellow, with patchy swaths of dusty gray. I am overcome with remorse at its discovery.

Why? Why did we forget about this bar of soap? When did we buy it? Who were we then, what were we doing, where were we going that day, that night, that week? Was Ira healthy when we bought this? What about Sam and me? This was bought before he fucked someone else—but when? What period of our lives? Before the Bear was born? If not, how big was she when it arrived in our home?

It is like discovering a time capsule left by our previous selves as proof that, once upon a time, we had the semblance of a life together. I want to show Sam this fragment we forsook and omitted for no reason other than selfish preoccupation with anything and everything else. Had we been more mindful, more grounded, more present, more simpatico, would we have been happy with what we had? Would we have ever allowed ourselves to become like that messy bathroom cabinet, where more and more junk accumulated and almost extinguished something so basic and pure as a bar of Ivory soap?

I begin to fantasize that the soap is a portal through which I can return to the era when it was bought to spend just a day inhabiting those former selves, before all the pain, before all the sickness, before all the side-fuckery. I see us so clearly in my mind: it's a beautiful Saturday in autumn, and we've gone for a walk, Sam, me, the Bear, Ira. We stroll down from Chelsea to the Village to hang in Washington Square Park, where we happen upon some street musicians playing Clifford Brown's "Joy Spring." We don't have a song, Sam and I; it's more like we have a series of songs that resonate and remind us of our connection, and "Joy Spring" is one of them. I take the Bear out of the stroller Ira is tied to, and as we dance, Sam takes pictures. I know, as he is snapping away, that those images will one day become iconic in our family photo album, ones we will always return to, even when the Bear is all grown with a family of her own. The music ends; we continue to amble through the Village, stopping for an early dinner of spaghetti carbonara at some Italian café with outdoor tables and a half-filled water bowl for patrons with dogs. I see us, laughing, passing the Bear back and forth between our laps, savoring the weather, the wine, our sweet little family.

In the twilight, wending our way home, we pop into a pharmacy to pick up some sundries—diapers, bottled water, Peanut M&M's, soap. And despite how vividly my mind can conjure the events leading up to these fanciful purchases, the reverie comes to an abrupt end when I try to impose how it was that we came to have that forgotten bar of soap. It's as though this is where some sort of higher power with a more acute sense of realism takes over, runs backstage, and brings down the curtain on my attempt to bullshit myself. Because, while we may have been those people who lived out a day like that at one time, it was never as carefree or fun or imbued with soft-focus tenderness as the one I was compelled to invent in my grief. It was as if, somewhere inside of me, I believed that only by embellishing a more halcyon version of the past could I feel justified in experiencing the full-throttle anguish of my present.

In truth, we were never those people in the daydream, dancing in the light of a golden afternoon in the park, basking in the promise of a multitude of days ahead that would be just like that one. We are the people who would leave the soap in the bathroom cabinet, the people who would leave the cake out in the rain. I think of that abandoned cake, melting in the dark, unable to be replicated, its recipe gone forever. I think, too, of the piece of our wedding cake we saved in our freezer for good luck during our first year of marriage—how we shared a freezer-burned bite on our first anniversary, gamely pretending it was as delicious as the day we'd wed, and how we had to discard it when we sold our house to move east.

"I can't bear to throw it away," Sam said. "I just wish we could keep it with us always . . ."

"There will be other cakes," I said, because I believed there would be—that there would always, always be cakes. Pulling him into my embrace, I kissed his cheeks, his nose, his lips. "We still have so much to celebrate."

And as I stand weeping in the bathroom, clutching that dingy, rectangular, barely recognizable token of our past, it begins to dawn on me that the loss of what one wishes had happened is just as painful, if not more so, than the loss of what has actually been. No, we may never have been those people in my figment, but oh my god, how we wanted to be. How very much we wanted to be. If only life were like memorizing a long monologue—you could stop when you made a mistake, go back to the beginning, and do it again and again until you got it right.

Dust from the wrapper adheres to my sweaty palm. The soap has become warm in my grasp. I give it one final, gentle squeeze, and then, though I really don't want to, I unfurl my fingers and let it go.

Eight

MIDNIGHT IN PARIS / MIDDAY IN CHELSEA

My remorse and shell shock over Sam's infidelity was such that, suddenly, after a hiatus of god knows how long, I began to sleep with him again. There was no premeditation or preamble; I basically just lunged at him one morning when he arrived from his sublet, as if I hoped to somehow *fuck him back* into the relationship. It wasn't a development I felt particularly good about, but I had taken to embracing my complicity in our relationship's demise and had run with it all the way to a land known as Batshit, Crazy. And in Batshit, Crazy, reason is governed by panic, and choice is fueled by abject fear.

Sam continued coming home before dawn, and when we were not getting it on, we would lie together in bed, wrapped in each other's arms while the Bear slept, none the wiser, in the other room. We continued to see Stephen, and Sam continued to be unable to tell me how long he would be "unsure" and whether—or when—he would stop fucking the chick from Miami.

"We could date," he offered during a Stephen session one day. "We could get together, you and I, for dates and see where it leads . . ."

My having taken up residence in the aforementioned Batshit made dating my own husband actually seem like a reasonable idea.

"OK," I said.

Stephen gently reminded me that it was counterintuitive for us to "work on" our marriage while Sam continued to "forge intimacy" with his sidepiece, but the most I could muster in response was a half-hearted shrug. I had been on the tightrope so long, I hadn't noticed that I was suddenly working without a net.

But where to go on a "date" with one's husband, who is currently sleeping (and eating steak) with another woman?

That was the question.

One idea I had was to visit one of our favorite special-occasion restaurants, because, let's face it, this was certainly a special occasion. I flipped through my mental file cabinet, but I kept coming up blank. Every place I thought of either was too expensive (which I thought might make Sam angry and uncomfortable) or no longer existed. More often than not, however, I would excitedly hit on a place from our history and, just as I did, I'd conjure the last time or the last several times—or, in some cases, *all of the times*—we had been there and remember that the experiences had been frankly not so great.

In the midst of my trying to figure out what to do, Sam sent me an email:

How about we go see the new Woody Allen movie?

Well.

This could not have been more perfect.

Woody Allen—or, more specifically, Woody Allen movies—was as intrinsic and specific to our love affair as the serviceable pepperoni pizza and warm white wine we'd had on our first rendezvous. Our entire early relationship rapport was built on one of us repeating a line from a Woody Allen movie and the other chiming in with its rejoinder. We could do entire scenes together without any prompting whatsoever. It was after we attended a screening of *Deconstructing Harry* that Sam told me for the first time that he loved me; the morning after he proposed, we watched *Annie Hall* and *Manhattan* back-to-back; the night we returned from our honeymoon, we watched *Crimes and Misdemeanors*. The last Woody Allen movie Sam and I had seen together was *Small Time Crooks*, eleven years ago. I pictured us, in that cavernous movie theater in Westwood, holding hands and sharing Raisinets in the dark. There would come a time when Woody Allen—his films, his dialogue, his role in our lives—would recede from view. Life went on; Woody Allen went on, making movies we didn't even see. Then the day would come that I would watch *Match Point* on cable by myself, and Sam would do the same with *Scoop*. I remembered how ruefully I'd greeted the news that he had seen it without me, how weirdly betrayed I'd felt while he tried to comfort me.

"I mean, it's not like I cheated on you," he had said.

If only I had known, I thought to myself, *how wonderful life was back then, when the biggest act of marital treachery perpetrated was taking in a film Roger Ebert reviewed as being leftover morsels of* Manhattan Murder Mystery *"after they've been strained through* The Curse of the Jade Scorpion.*"*

Be that as it may, we were long overdue for Woody Allen—even lesser Woody Allen. This was abundantly clear.

The plan was that we'd hit the noon screening at the Chelsea Clearview Cinemas right down the street from our apartment, then go home to the Bear, and then, after we played for a bit, I'd cook us all a big pot of spaghetti carbonara for an early dinner.

The Woody Allen movie in question, *Midnight in Paris*, was one of those Woody Allen–less Woody Allen movies, where a (usually/ obviously) goyish guy stands in for Woody, awkwardly deploying all his nebbishy tics and stammers. The prospect of a Woody Allen–less Woody Allen movie didn't bother me per se; I had enjoyed John Cusack pinch-hitting for him in *Bullets Over Broadway*, and one of my very favorites, *The Purple Rose of Cairo*, despite being absent of Woody himself, was replete with his voice and sensibility. People were raving about *Midnight* being the best Woody Allen movie in years, and yet, as exciting as that was, all I cared about was that Sam had been the one who'd thought of it. For some reason, this, and this alone, buoyed my optimism. *He still remembers,* I kept thinking. *He still remembers when we were an "us" who loved the same things. This bodes well; he wants me, he wants us . . .*

I wanted to look pretty. I had lost a bunch of weight since I'd first learned of the affair, but not in a good way. I had virtually no appetite, and my innards felt as if they were taking an advanced spin class twenty-four hours a day. Clothes hung about my wasting body, and my shoulders were so scrawny that they were beginning to resemble a BMX handlebar. The teensiest layer of body fat, having not received word from the rest of my evaporating body, cocooned my form, holding on tight, just in case I ever got my life back. Mostly, though, what I looked was nervous, as if the man with whom I'd be spending this time were a stranger and not my husband of twelve years.

Sitting in front of the mirror, readying myself to see Sam—to see Woody Allen–less Woody Allen—and trying in vain to mask aubergine under-eye circles, I fixated on unplayed scenes: variants of us together in the future, just as we had been in the past, quoting lines from the films we loved while holding hands on walks or drives, lying in bed, what have you. I further imagined how we would explain, in this halcyon time to come, our impasse, the minor blip in our marriage when Sam took to fucking a Floridian who made him steak and salad. We'd be happy—maybe a little smug, but not too much—about having beaten the statistical norm of adultery and separation and grave, grave unrest, to find each other again on the other side of the shit-storm.

"Yes, it was a fucked-up time, but invaluable, transformative . . ." we'd repeat to other rapt couples, whose hidden troubles would suddenly feel not just workable but almost welcome if they could lead to similar relationship Nirvana. "We would not be who we have become without that time; those terrible, terrifying moments led us to something truly divine, and as hard as it was, we wouldn't trade it for anything . . ."

We go to the movie. It's the middle of the day in the middle of the week in the middle of Chelsea. The theater is mostly empty, except for the usual suspects: old people, gays, old gays. We settle in, and right off the bat, it's . . . weird. I find myself making small talk—not the kind I'd make with my partner who I know loves me, but the kind I'd maybe make with some rando I met online who I strongly suspect rues the moment he saw my profile and swiped right. I am out of my skinny/fat body, floating above the musty Chelsea Clearview seats, and I watch myself being all faux breezy and chatty about various inanities, trying to fill the void so that neither of us notices how not OK this all feels. We do not hold hands; we do not share Raisinets. We both have small Cokes. I don't normally drink Coke, but I am trying to *do* things, change the *landscape*; be as *one*. My incessant chattiness begins to wane, the previews begin, I sip my Coke. The sweet syrup momentarily takes me back to my childhood, when I enjoyed the occasional Coke, when Coke was a "special treat" only for dinners out. I would have to nurse my "special treat" to make it last—there would be only one Coke to be had, after all.

"You look at the bill and see—that's where they get you," my father would admonish. "The drinks . . ."

We sit through the endless overamplified previews, but my mind is elsewhere, consumed, for some reason, with vague memories of the "New Coke" controversy of the 1980s. The Coca-Cola Company, as I recall, had come up with a new, "improved" recipe, and though taste tests had proved people actually preferred it, when the changes were put into effect, the public was outraged and a backlash ensued. What the powers that be failed to realize was that, in the end, people didn't really want "new"; they wanted what they remembered.

I can relate; I want what I remember, too.

And try though I do, as I sip my Coke, I simply can't conjure anything except for the immediate, the right here, the right-now experience of a cloyingly sweet drink, the carbonation of which, a bit too jacked, is burning the back of my tongue.

The movie begins. Owen Wilson plays a screenwriter / aspiring novelist who travels to Paris on a vacation with his fiancée (played by Rachel McAdams) and her parents. Despite their impending nuptials, it is clear that their relationship sucks. One night, Owen Wilson gets drunk, hops into a vintage Peugeot, and travels back in time to the Paris of the 1920s, where he meets (and is befriended by) members of the "Lost Generation." The glitterati are, of course, not presented as they actually *were*, but as quintessential versions, as what Owen Wilson wants them to be. In short order, he falls in love with them, with the epoch, and with Marion Cotillard.

The usual Woody Allen tropes are trotted out: nostalgia, Hollywood-bashing, insufferable pseudo-intellectuals who claim to know everything but know nothing (or who know less than Allen or, in this case, his proxy). There are sexy backdrops, high production values, and A-list celebrities in the kinds of minor roles they play only for the chance to have "Woody Allen" on their résumé.

Owen Wilson is the classic Woody Allen protagonist: he's a schlemiel, he is talented (we are endlessly told), and his serial self-deprecation feels slightly disingenuous. Then there's Rachel McAdams. Unlike the heroines of Woody Allen yore, this leading lady is not kooky but charming with bone structure (Mia Farrow), nor is she kooky but charming with singular style (Diane Keaton). Instead, she is a materialistic shrew with, well, awful parents. She seems to care not a whit that Owen Wilson would be infinitely happier if his work satisfied him—if he could realize his dreams of becoming a novelist—because she finds his aspirations silly. She doesn't give a shit about his "art"; she wants to live in fucking Malibu.

I find myself cringing in my seat at this lazily drawn basic-bitch Flat Stanley with nothing whatsoever to redeem her. Worse, I sense not only that Sam loathes her but that when he looks at her, he sees me, and when he looks at her and Owen Wilson, he sees us.

"*Don't do it, man—don't get married,*" I imagine him imploring Owen's character. "*Wives* suck—*and I don't mean in a good way. . .*"

Of all the Woody Allen movies we could see in this moment—of all the possible fictitious dynamics we could be bearing witness to—why, *why*, did it have to be this? OK, so not everything can be *Annie Hall* levels of charming love affair, but could we not expect, or at the very least hope, for the whimsically offbeat ardor of a *Hannah and Her Sisters* or a *Broadway Danny Rose*?

"I prefer his 'early, funny' films," I whisper to Sam, referring to one of the lines from *Stardust Memories* with which we often amused each other. I am trying for levity, trying—while this train wreck of a relationship playing out on the screen threatens to derail every last iota of our jaunt—to remind Sam of not just the way Woody Allen was but the way *we* were.

The Way We Were.

Jesus, I think to myself. *Talk about movies that don't end well. Even Katie and Hubbell could not—despite their love, despite being best friends—find their way back to each other. He was never going to write that novel; she was never not going to rabble-rouse; they were never going to move to France.*

Sam shrugs.

"He doesn't really do that kind anymore . . ."

No, I think to myself. *He doesn't.* Gone are the days of Woody Allen's "early, funny" movies; he's moved on, changed partners, changed leading ladies, married his de facto stepdaughter, been embroiled in sexual abuse allegations involving his adopted child. What was once attractive, hilarious, smart, fresh, and original now strikes me as sad, occasionally mean, and—given the details of Woody's real life—more than a little creepy.

There was a time when his work mollified me, when I related completely to his worldview and felt there could never be a better urban poet for the anxiety-prone. That nasal, Brooklyn-inflected voice was a balm to the tired, the lovelorn, the tortured souls who slogged it out every damn day on streets and subways, in restaurants, and in the overheated shoeboxes we called home. It was a voice that spoke to every last one of us who was riddled with guilt and self-doubt and questions for which there could never be definitive answers.

"I know exactly how you feel," Woody Allen seemed to say with electrifying candor in every picture, every jazz-infused frame. "I know exactly how you feel to wonder the point of this thing called life and its seemingly endless parade of pain and suffering."

And by the end of the roughly 120 minutes, he would bring me to the edge of whatever my latest what's-the-use-tinged despair was, only to point out that no matter how bleak it all was, salvation could be found simply by wandering into a screening of *Duck Soup.*

I had believed him.

Facile and glib though his assertion may have been, there is still a piece of me that continues to hold fast to it. I am, after all, in a movie theater with my estranged husband, seeking reminders of who we are and what we have, trying to lose ourselves in the art we love, that transports us, that makes us feel whole again and like we should never give up. I am, like Woody Allen, fetishizing the past: I am longing for the movies of my youth, the days when my dog was healthy, the life I lived prior to knowing of my husband's affair. I am locked in a bizarre sort of purgatory, wherein I can fixate only on years I have lived before the one in which I exist currently and on fantasies of the ones in my future. This affliction, along with my strong dislike of the movie, makes me dizzy, and I begin to perspire, despite the theater's overzealous air-conditioning game.

The movie ends. The credits roll. We stay to watch them out of habit more than interest.

We amble home. Sam takes Ira out. I relieve the sitter and make the carbonara.

"What was the movie about?" the Bear asks over dinner.

"It's about this guy," I tell her, "who goes to Paris and finds a special car that lets him time-travel to the 1920s, which is many years before the movie takes place."

"Oooh—does he have fun?"

"He does have fun: he meets all of his idols, and they're nice to him and tell him the book he's writing is good, and he really likes them. And then he meets a lady who's very beautiful, and he kind of falls in love with her."

"Is she a princess?"

"No—but she's very nice . . ."

"Do they get married?"

"No—"

"He doesn't marry her," Sam interjects, "but she helps him realize that he's about to make a big mistake."

"What's the 'big mistake'?" the Bear asks.

"That he was going to marry this *other* lady . . ."

"Why?"

"Why what?"

"Why is it a mistake?"

"Because she doesn't make him happy."

"Why not?" the Bear wants to know.

There is an uncomfortable pause. In the silence, I feel annoyingly compelled to defend the heinous Rachel McAdams character, but I swallow this urge instead of the pasta I am not eating. I notice that Sam is also not eating his pasta.

"Is there something the matter with the food?" I ask Sam, changing the subject.

"No—why?"

"Why doesn't the lady make him happy?" the Bear asks, returning to the subject.

"Because you've barely touched it," I say to Sam.

"I ate it; I think I'm just full . . ."

"Full of what?" I ask. "Steak?"

"Nancy—"

"Shit?"

"Hey!" the Bear shouts gleefully. "That's a naughty word!"

"This is not OK." Sam seethes.

He's right, of course, but I am already in the zone; my entire being is buzzing, and I am finally not just sad or bereft or longing—I'm furious.

"No, it's not—it's not OK," I say, getting up and snatching his plate and mine from the table. "Maybe if you hadn't filled up on steak and salad and whatever the fuck else, you'd have an appetite."

I stomp off to the kitchen and begin scraping our almost totally full plates into the trash. As I do, I hear the Bear begin to giggle.

"Mom said *two* naughty words!"

I had made a promise to myself to shield the Bear from our conflicts, and now, having abandoned this vow, I briefly consider using one of our fancy Wüsthof knives for self-evisceration. Instead, I begin cleaning the dishes. Slowly, I come down off my rage high. My feelings veer from self-abasement to self-righteousness and back at an alarming clip.

Though I really didn't care for it, I seem to not be able to get *Midnight in Paris* off my mind. I keep replaying the ending, where Owen Wilson decides that—the allure of bygone days notwithstanding—living in the present is most optimal. I find myself debating which is worse: pining for something you once had but that is now lost, or longing for something you are only just now realizing you *never had* but *wanted* and *still want desperately?*

We cannot be transported. We cannot be made whole again. We cannot go back.

Woody Allen isn't the same, and neither are we. It strikes me that *Midnight in Paris*—a movie I thought had been a terrible choice—had in fact granted me the sort of psychic shoulder-shaking I needed to peer over the railing and into the moonless canyon of my denial. Because the Truth—the Big, Bad, Scary Truth—that had been so obscured by the shadow of my intense need to control the narrative and make it happy and positive, make all the bad shit befalling us not true, had, in the pitch black of the Chelsea Clearview Cinemas on Twenty-Third Street, been illuminated as if by klieg light. No, there would be no vintage Peugeot to ferry us to a better period. The stiff cocktail I'd ingested of time with a splash of coping mechanism had managed to alter my memory of my life with Sam—the places we'd dined, the desultory times we'd shared in those places—so much that I wasn't actually nostalgic for what we'd once had but for that which had never existed.

Nine

LADIES OF THE COVEN

It is close to three a.m., a little over a week after the movie "date." I am on the phone with my friend Charity, a gonzo journalist with little tolerance for men who stray. This is the third time this week Charity has counseled me in the middle of the night, and she is doing so with as much sensitivity as she can muster—which is a terrific struggle for someone whose volume, even in repose, is set to "outrage."

"Stop the madness, Brenda!" Charity roars. "Get his dick out of your eyehole already!"

A platinum blonde with a mind as sharp as a Kikuichi knife, Charity storms through life rocking a marcel wave, head-to-toe leather, and a scowl.

"You there, Brenda? Give a moan or two so I know you're still alive and I don't need to call in the SWAT team . . ."

"Brenda": my very special Charity-bestowed nickname inspired by the gravelly-voiced actress Brenda Vaccaro, whom she insists I sound like and who, in the Playtex commercials of our youth, implored us to use tampons "intelligently," I guess because so many women had been using them *dumbly*.

"Yes," I say finally. "I'm here."

"You're too good for this, dude," Charity brays. "About *a million times* too good for this. Get. The. Fuck. Away. From. Him. I can't even *believe* when he brought up the idea of 'dating' you didn't leap across the couch and strangle him. I would have. I would have kicked that little shit into a coma for you."

I am not one for violence, and yet her words are both a balm and a buttress: each time Charity paints a new picture of beating my husband and his wandering peen into a bloody pulp, my heart swells like the Grinch's at the end, when he finally gets what Christmas is about.

"I swear to fuck," she continues. "You remind me of my Christian Scientist grandmother. She was never sick until she had cancer, but her *paradigm* her entire life was to be just outrageously, pleasantly in denial of all sickness. So, she just Christian Science-d that shit away in her head and never told anyone, because medicine (and doctors and all that crap) was *too unclean* and she wasn't going to do it, she just wasn't. So . . . she died. Because she wanted to keep her head in the clouds. Don't be like her. Don't. Die. Get on your combat boots and fight."

Unfortunately, I can't find it in me to "fight." My whole being embodies tiredness and restlessness in equal measure: I can't move, and yet I also can't sit still. I want to crawl out of my body, slither across the room like a snake, liquefy, and then seep through the floorboards into my downstairs neighbor's apartment. She is a hoarder, and I imagine my condensed remains will go unnoticed among the detritus forever.

Charity rages on; she segues seamlessly back and forth from the subject of my marital *mishegoss* into rants about the cult of celebrity, the nexus between politics and fashion, the patriarchy, autoerotic asphyxiation, and the *I Ching*.

In the spaces between these subjects, I think of our friendship over these past seven years, forged over the course of umpteen meals shared "family style" in eateries all over Manhattan and Brooklyn. From the get-go, Charity was *kemosabe*—one of my most cherished writer friends—championing my work, reading pages anytime I asked, and making editorial suggestions that consistently blew my mind with their incisiveness. We became a mutual admiration society of like-minded Libras, born only one day apart, feting each other within days of those dates every year, toasting each other with white Burgundy wines that had dragons on the labels.

But as the previous year folded into the present one, and my life became more and more unhappy, I found myself pulling away. It wasn't her, and it wasn't conscious—just more of my pathological need to keep up appearances. The old "show must go on" mentality, compounded by my dread of being perceived as a failure, fueled an insatiable need to keep my troubles, whatever they were, under wraps. All my life, people had seemed to feel comfortable admitting their fiascos and foibles to me, but no matter my calamity, when it struck, I'd betray none of it, becoming, instead, remarkably and uncharacteristically taciturn. Thus, it made perfect sense that I told basically no one, including Charity, of my marital woes—certainly not explicitly—up to and including the "temporary" separation. But by Easter, when I began turning down social invitations and ignoring messages and emails, Charity gently took me to task, asking me to explain the reasons behind my disappearing act. Way before I was able to metabolize it all myself—and before I was able to divulge the truth of it all to anyone else—I came clean to Charity about what was happening with Sam and me.

"I think that when you're neurotic, it's because you are so frightened of your own pain, you will literally scuttle everything in your life to avoid dealing with yourself," she told me after she'd finally cajoled me out of my shame cave and into a West Chelsea bar near my pad.

"I know I've been like this," she said, pausing briefly before glancing past me to watch the taxis and buses and cars hurtling by on Tenth Avenue. "Still am. It's like you sacrifice everyone else in your life to your own cowardice in this self-perpetuating stunt your brain pulls. And at a certain point, you just have to deal with your own lameness and start building your ego from the rubble."

"How do I begin?" I asked her.

"You already have, Brenda," she told me. "You already fucking have."

She had essentially scraped me off the floor and strapped me into the Cyclone ride I'd thought was much too terrifying by assuring me that (a) I could do it and that (b) I needn't do it alone. And now Charity—this badass female who truly gives less than a scintilla of a fuck what anyone thinks of her—in addition to refusing to let me slip away from *her*, also refuses to let me slip through those big, bad aforementioned cracks in the floor. If in the past Charity's energy could unnerve or even drain, it now makes me feel as if I have the full-throttle protection of a Praetorian fleet.

Over the course of this year and for the next several afterward, Charity is to become my best be-all-end-all port in the storm, advising me at all hours from her aerie in DUMBO. These conversations will generally take place between midnight and six a.m. because Charity hails from San Francisco, and though she's lived in New York for over a decade, she never got around to adjusting either her internal clock or the ones in her home, remaining instead perennially on Pacific Standard Time. This bit of providence not only makes her endlessly available to me *emotionally*, it makes her available *practically*: if I happen to find myself on the brink of psychic collapse at, say, one in the morning, Charity is invariably up because, as far as she's concerned, it's ten p.m. the previous day.

On this particular late night, I am completely out of sorts, am shaken to the core, do not know which way is up or down, want to die, but the fact that I have a child and a dog prevents me from exploring this as a viable option. Sam and I, despite our disastrous "date," are still engaging in the same twisted dance, still pushing and pulling, on-again, off-again, making believe that the tempest we are braving is in fact a sunshiny day worthy of a picnic in the park. In saner moments, I can see it; I can own my part in the delusion. But just the same, I can't seem to quit him. I have called Charity to enlist her help, to glean some wisdom, to have her inspire my ire. She, as usual, rises to the occasion.

"Sweetie, I am so sorry this fuck-tard is hurting you this way. Makes me so furious. *But please just don't help him.* He no longer deserves to be in your bed *or* your body. No. More. It is self-sabotage by proxy. It is corruption of the quintessence, soul suicide by self-appointed cop, sleeping with the enemy, feminist tropes of the like."

Charity punctuates this litany by ferociously exhaling her cigarette, and I imagine her as the fire-breathing dragon in *Beowulf.*

As she continues to rant about the "sexual apartheid" and "how our psyches have become this unremitting Sartre play" and something-something about "being bitch-slapped by our own internalized Gloria Steinems," I watch Ira sleeping beside me. His right paw, shaved and bruised from where there had been a needle from the IV used during his last transfusion, rests on my right hip. In the bruise, I see what looks like the face of Winston Churchill. Ira breathes slowly, and with each exhale there is a slight whistle, like the sound of a teapot beginning to boil in another room or a sleeper train rounding a bend in the distance.

"Ira is dying," I say finally. "And I can't help but think he's hanging on cuz he's afraid to leave me this way."

"I thought you said he was doing better."

"He is . . . ," I say.

"Wagging his tail, eating?" Charity asks. "Still happily taking dumps in front of Sarah Jessica Parker's town house?"

"He is," I say again. "But for how long? I just don't get why everything that's happening to me is happening all at once."

"Cramped nests," Charity declares. "The Universe often likes to kick us out of them and into the nth degree of fuckery to prove a point."

I nod as if Charity, all the way in Brooklyn, can see me. I can hear her puttering around her kitchen, uncorking a bottle of what must be one of the many Sancerres that line the bottom of her fridge, then lighting another cig.

"Lissen to me, Brenda," she says, taking a quick drag. "I'm sorry about sweet Ira, truly, truly. And I think you're right: he wants to make sure you're cool; he wants to know that you are OK to help yourself. But here's my Rx: You need to meditate on the wrathful goddesses. Get some Shakti in you. Call on Durga, Kali, Yamuna—all them bitches. They're in you anyway; you just have to call them forth."

I nod again and sigh heavily.

"Things'll get better, babe, they really will. I believe that. But first, as with anything, you have to be the change you want to see, yes?"

"I guess I'm not sure *what* exactly that is," I say. "Or the change that I want *changes*. The minute I think I know I've had it—it's over, I'm done—he *does* something or *says* something, or *we* do something that makes me think, 'No, there's a shred of hope, there really is. And if I could just do *x*, *y*, and *z*, or get *him* to do or see *x*, *y*, and *z* . . . or maybe it's that *x* is not possible, but who cares, because *y* and *z* are more than most people get, so hang in, keep trying, keep going, read this book, do that thing.' And then it just all goes south again, and I'm back at the beginning."

"I hear you," she says. "It's like *Hamlet*, with hate-fucking."

I consider this for a second.

"But is it really *hate*? I mean, maybe it's that we're finally ready to give each other the love we both want so badly, but we got locked into a bad pattern and don't quite know how to get out of it."

"Doubtful," she says. "Too much about it that reeks of desperation. Too much ego involved."

"I suppose I *am* pretty disgusted at myself for how useful an aphrodisiac adultery has been."

"Don't do that to yourself, Brenda."

"You know, when I first found out about him and the chick from Miami, one of the things that just killed me was the image of him fucking this other woman while wearing his wedding ring. I just couldn't let it go. So I confront him about it: 'You fuck another woman while you're wearing your wedding ring? The wedding ring that indicates you're a married man, married to me?' And he goes: 'No—*I take it off*.'"

"Married men should never remove their wedding rings—" Charity snaps.

"He takes it off before he fucks her!"

"Unless they work with a lathe or something, but even then—"

"Like, part of his pre-sex 'prep' is removing the evidence that he is married, despite the fact that this chick *knows* he's married. I don't know why this disturbs me more than anything else. More than, you know, the other day in therapy him saying that he's 'afraid of losing me' but at the same time saying he wants to be 'free.' Or that he's renewed his sublet at least through August. Or that he's always enraged with me and seems generally contemptuous of me, our life, his responsibilities. And, oh yeah, that he refuses to stop *shtupping* Miss Miami."

"Good lord—"

"Is there anything about this that's workable?"

"Sure. Provided you give up 100 percent of your needs, your expectations, and your humanity."

"I just can't seem to shake the idea that there must be something— *something I'm not doing or haven't thought of . . . something to make him see . . .* to make him want to fight for this, too."

"Unfortunately, you don't have the power to *make him* do anything. You're not 'the Douche Whisperer,' Brenda."

Power, I think to myself. I try to imagine what such a thing would feel like right now, what it might look like, how it would change me. There were times, fleeting moments in the past, when I'd felt what it was to have power. But in almost every one of those instances, I'd barely had time to bask in its brawny caress before it was gone. Now, in its all-too-familiar dearth, I begin to turn my attention to ways I might till the fertile soils from which such facility could spring forth. *Charity is right,* I think to myself: I'm not "the Douche Whisperer," nor do I want anymore to "whisper" when what's called for is a roar. I need to stop with the magical thinking and start enacting my own particular brand of magic. But I need help with this. *The time has come,* I tell myself, *to pay a visit to Enchantments, the place to which I have fled at just about every end-of-my-tether, mojo-less juncture in my life.* I briefly describe Enchantments and its tatted-up cabal of witchery's best and brightest, and Charity agrees to ride shotgun.

We are off to see the witches.

A few sleepless hours later, I am rushing across Twenty-Third Street toward Enchantments, and my last audience with the Ladies of the Coven pushes through the intervening seven years to the forefront of my thoughts. As if by cosmic treadmill, I am right there, smack in the middle of my in vitro vortex, hopped up on more hormones than a circa-1970 supermarket chicken, the ticking of my biological clock having assumed the incessancy of a Bergman film. I see a woman emotionally and physically exhausted from the myriad drugs, needles, and hospital visits. Her husband, meanwhile, has sunk into a deep and debilitating depression.

I see the two of us, limping around our one-room Meatpacking pad in abject, bitter silence, the miasma of despair emanating from the four corners of our home like a noxious gas that lifts us until we are airborne and begin to drift apart. And the more we drift, the more stress continues to engulf us and the more divergent our responses: For Sam, the toll of our failure makes him recoil into a morose ball of nihilistic conjecture, in which he repeatedly questions whether it makes sense to continue—with fertility treatments or with life in general. I, on the other hand, overwhelmed with an even greater zeal to realize my dream of becoming a mother, throw myself into achieving said goal with nary a pause to consider how it might impact my body, my psyche, my partner, or our relationship.

This scene dissolves into another, and I see us somewhat later, after the second IVF attempt. We take a walk, I feel dizzy, we go back, I lie down. Later, I pee on a stick, and instantly, in the blank white square, two blue lines beam into view. Can it be? I pee on another and another and another: blue-blue, blue-blue, blue-blue. *I'm. Pregnant. Preg-nant. Preg-nancy!* I scream, I dance, I cry. The triumph of this thoroughly ecstatic moment is short-lived: Sam, *unfortunately*, does not quite share my elation. In fact, just after the first pee stick comes up positive, he has an epiphany: he's not so sure he wants to be a father.

"I don't think I'm ready for this," he says.

"What are you saying?" I ask. "It's what we've always wanted."

"No," he tells me. "I don't think it is what *I* wanted. It's what *you* wanted. And I guess what *I* wanted was . . . for you to be happy."

So you can imagine how thrilled he is when we get to my first ob-gyn appointment and the doctor tells us it's twins.

Even for me, wrapping my mind around what my doctor refers to as "two for the price of one" is a bit of a challenge, given my husband's attitude and our imploding marriage. Still, I am incredibly excited and can't quite believe my luck. And sure enough, my luck will run out: toward the end of my first trimester, prenatal testing will reveal that something is wrong—very wrong. I am told that while "Baby B" tested as healthy, "Baby A" is afflicted with a fatal abnormality known as triploidy and will likely die in utero or within minutes of birth in the dubious event it even makes it to term. Worse, if "Baby A" perishes in utero, there is an enormous risk of miscarrying the entire pregnancy, thus putting in peril the life and viability of "Baby B."

"People have 'reductions' all the time," my doctor says, as I sit shell-shocked in her office, listening to her explain my options.

Reduction, I think. *What a terrible, bullshit euphemism. And if it's supposed to make me feel better about what I'm electing to do, it doesn't.*

I know exactly what I am doing, and I resent the medical establishment's ham-fisted attempts at poetry . . .

As I cross First Avenue at Ninth Street, the scene in my mind fast-forwards six months: moments after Christo and Jeanne-Claude's *The Gates* is unfurled in Central Park, the Bear is born. If Sam's ambivalence toward me remains, with respect to the Bear it has vanished. From the moment of her first breath, he is completely obsessed—the most loving daddy imaginable. I watch them that first night after her birth, Sam standing by the hospital window, cradling the swaddled Bear, both of them framed by the fading blue winter light, Christo and Jeanne-Claude's magnificent saffron-colored fabric panels waving languidly in the background. And I am so very glad I persevered, that I did not give up, that I knew, in my heart, that in the end Sam would be happy. And I hope that, someday, he will come to view it this way, too.

In the months that follow the Bear's birth, as I recover from the C-section and the emotional whiplash of the prior year, the unimaginable pain of what transpired will begin to fade into the distance. The only tangible relic left from my numerous attempts to conjure a child will be the remains of the fertility candle. I will save those splotches of aromatic wax flecked with glitter in a Mexican ceramic box on my vanity, peering in from time to time to visit what's left of my magic. Because I know there will come a day when I will need to make more.

~

It is a full house when I arrive at Enchantments, as we are within days of Litha, the Wiccan festival celebrating the summer solstice. The joint is teeming with witches hoping to stock up before that annual moment when the sun is at the height of its power before its gradual slide into darkness. I look around the shop. Nothing has changed: still the rough-hewn wood floors, still the shelves holding herbs with names like deer's tongue and devil's shoestring, still the air thick with the scent of frankincense and myrrh. Charity accompanies me to the back, and beneath a WHERE THERE'S A WITCH THERE'S A WAY bumper sticker, a high priestess named Heather holds out a tarot deck and tells me to ask a question.

How do I save my marriage?

Heather shuffles the deck and fans it across a crooked wooden table for me to pull ten cards. The three of us pause to take in the spread. One of the cards—"the Tower"—catches my eye. I examine the image: a gray edifice being struck by lightning, terrified-looking people diving from its windows. It looks like the worst card anyone has ever received, *ever*, something I point out to Heather.

"Not necessarily," Heather says. "Think of the card as an allegory: storm clouds brewing, waves crashing, fires raging, people falling. It's crazy intense—everything's moving around superfast, *except for*"—she points to the card—"the Tower. The Tower stays stuck."

"Sounds like my husband," I say. "Stuck in all the ways he's pissed at me."

Heather shakes her head.

"This is about you—not him. And something you've never been able to let go of or move past."

I look back down at this most ominous of cards.

"You need to figure out what that is," she says.

I nod.

"And," she adds, "once you figure out the 'what,' you need to ask yourself *why*."

And for the second time this day, I board the cosmic treadmill. Once again, I am in the midst of the in vitro vortex, only this time there is no prelude, no fast-forward, no end. The only scene on the bill is the one my mind omitted earlier. It is something I have held on to, but unlike the wax shards in the pretty little box, these are remnants I have refused, until now, to visit:

It is the day of the "reduction." I am alone at the hospital; Sam has fled for the hills of western Massachusetts to attend a four-day "silence retreat."

I am led to a room, where I undress and put on a robe of indeterminate color. *Is it gray,* I wonder, *or blue?* I look around at the room, the floor, my arm, my hand. Everything is the same: everything is either gray or blue here.

A technician comes in, then the doctor. In the semidarkness, I lie down on a table between them. The procedure is quick, and I remain awake, with my head turned away from the ultrasound monitor the doctor uses to guide the instrument into "Baby A's" heart. When it's over, the doctor has me turn back so that, for the first time, she can show me "Baby B."

My baby.

My Bear, "Baby B."

The light emanating from the screen is like a bright moon, and as I watch "Baby B," a tiny tadpole dancing in a snowstorm, tears I think will never end cascade down my cheeks and into my ears.

Later, in a recovery room, clutching an ultrasound photo of "Baby B," I hear Bette Midler's "From a Distance" wafting down the hallway from a technician's easy-listening radio station. And as I lie on that table, listening to a song about the way things seem versus the way things actually are, my thoughts turn to my husband. I think of how, shortly after we learned of our fertility problems, he took me to see Bette in concert at Madison Square Garden. I think of how moved I was by his attempt to cheer me; how much I loved him for tearing up during Bette's performance of this tune. Despite the chasm and all that has transpired, I *still* love Sam. And I cannot imagine a life without him. Yet, in this moment, I can also no longer imagine a life with him. Certainly not the life we'd had.

Bette continues to sing; I begin to think about the inevitability of decisions. Awful, difficult, wrenching decisions. Decisions you try to avoid. Decisions that are final and unambiguous and that do not, in any way, reflect your wishes or dreams. Decisions that reach inside, grab you by your innards, and shake you so vigorously that your entire being is flipped inside out. Decisions that, in the end, don't feel like decisions at all, like the one that has me lying on this table. I think of the Scarecrow in *The Wizard of Oz* telling Dorothy, who's arrived at a crossroads, that "some people go both ways." But how does one "go both ways" without splitting off, literally dividing in half before proceeding unwhole? I couldn't quite know then, as I lay in that room, that there would come a time when it would seem perfectly plausible to me to venture forth in two different directions, nor could I know then that the process of the same had already begun.

When I return from my reverie, I am filled with deep regret. Luckily, I am not alone; not only are Heather and Charity there, but the aforementioned bevy of sorceresses, too, who begin, one by one, to convene around us. And in the tiny antechamber where my reading is taking place, I begin to lay bare the ways in which I had avoided examining myself and my inner life, the way I had withdrawn into the sort of mute apathy I had once observed in the housewives of 1970s Connecticut. The ways I had told myself that it was Sam who had abdicated responsibility to me, to us, to our family, that it was Sam who had skipped out on our life, our commitment, our vows, and was soothing himself with his sidepiece from Miami while I lay in bed reading books like *How One of You Can Bring the Two of You Together*. But now, face-to-face with my cards, myself, my truth, I had no other choice but to reinsert the part of the story that had been, up to now, too painful to consider—the part of me that could easily have fallen into bed with another man, an acquaintance with whom I commenced a not-so-chaste email relationship shortly after the Bear's first birthday. So nothing ever *really* happened—my feelings of guilt for the myriad fantasies of having hot sex in hotel rooms and for spending a multitude of insomniac hours writing and responding to carefully crafted emails that balanced the appropriate and inappropriate on the edge of a knife are not assuaged. All that time I spent willingly theorizing about my "frigidity," yet somehow omitting, not just to Sam but to myself, that there was a time in our marriage when my days and nights were rife with daydreams of my email partner and me engaging in the sort of stylized, lush, and passionate affair Anouk Aimée had with her race car–driver lover in *A Man and a Woman*. But not only was I not French; I was also not one for subterfuge or secret meetings or shameful encounters of mind-blowing intensity, after which gray doom, confusion, and compartmentalization would follow—it wasn't even remotely my "brand." Shutting it all down before there was any serious e-scalation was easy: I told myself that the whole thing was merely a response to all the torment and alienation of the infertility and pregnancy. But what got buried along with this episode was the fact that it made me remember parts of myself that had long been forgotten. Maybe this is what happened for Sam, too. My focus became about Sam's ambivalence toward me, without any consideration of my own about him. I'm like "the Tower," stuck in time, stuck on my own inability to relinquish my feelings of rage, hurt, extreme disappointment—toward this man who was my husband, my partner, and my friend. Was it not possible that I not only had never forgiven Sam but also hadn't even realized this was a thing that needed to happen in order for us to move on? Could I? Could I forgive him? And if not, could I let him go?

One of the witches suggests that I need some "uncrossing magic" in the form of a candle, one that will offer me "divine protection." She custom-carves a candle with a switchblade, then anoints it with two insanely fragrant oils: "Crucible of Courage" on the shaft and "Clarity" on the wick. "Remember," Heather says as she wraps the finished candle in newspaper, "'uncrossing' is not a passive activity; it requires will."

I nod.

Heather puts her hands on my shoulders and gives them a reassuring squeeze.

"You will get through this time just fine, particularly if you remember that you already have inside you all the resources you need to deal with life and to do what you need to do."

Outside, Charity sits on the stoop next to Enchantments and has a smoke. I join her, putting the bundle with my candle between us and sitting for a minute, in the twilight, looking across the way and into the tiny shops that stretch out along Ninth Street.

"I'm afraid of being sad for the rest of my life," I tell her.

"I know, Bren. I know. But grief is finite if you're not avoiding it—if you just bravely face it head-on and allow yourself to feel the whole nut of it. You are more than capable of this. You have no idea how different your life is gonna look five years from now. It'll be a whole 'nother world, Bren . . ."

Charity picks up my bundle and puts it into her lap. She scoots closer and puts her arm around me.

"You really do remind me of my grandmother." She sighs. "You always have. She just couldn't let the fight into her head."

We walk to the corner, where I put Charity into a taxi. After I close her door, she rolls down the window. "I am totally 100 percent here for you—anytime," she says. "Call any hour. Say nothing; just heave sobs into the phone. Tell me what you need, and you will have anything I can give you—always."

The cab pulls away, and I watch it bounce toward the Brooklyn Bridge for a while before stuffing my bundle under my arm and rushing toward home.

Ten

JONATHAN

There was a woolly little hobbit of a man named Jonathan, who had lived in the West Village, right around the corner from Ciruela, in the same rent-controlled apartment, for decades. Jonathan was there long before the bankers and hedge-funders, before the fancy coffee joints and organic juice bars, before the double strollers and myriad Marc Jacobs boutiques. Jonathan's tenure harkened back to a time when the West Village was pretty much the exclusive terrain of gay men, when the fanciest, most la-di-da fuck-all place to have coffee was the delightfully ramshackle Caffè Sha-Sha on Hudson Street. Jonathan was intelligent and abrasive, a typical old-school, rabble-rousing Jewish lefty, for whom belligerence—particularly in political debate—was tantamount to foreplay. He was an editor for a small press, was on the board of ACT UP, and made sure that everyone who met him was fully aware of two things: he had graduated from Yale, and he was a Scorpio.

Despite Ciruela's relative proximity to his pad, Jonathan happened upon it only by chance, after picking up his Ambien and Lunesta scripts at the now-defunct discount pharmacy on Eighth Avenue. It was one of those late-March days when the temperature hovers around fifty-five degrees and the whole city, feeling the promise of spring, bounds out of their rimy burrows with collective enthusiasm and good cheer. Ciruela had just opened for the night. Monty was tending bar, and, as always, there were already plenty of good-looking boys adorning the stools, slurping sangria and Albariño and snacking on olives. As Jonathan passed the window, clutching his bag of dolls, he couldn't resist the gaggle of gays he beheld behind the glass, and he wandered in. Soon he was a regular, showing up each day at five fifteen on the dot, to spend the happiest of happy hours basking in the transient love of his fellow revelers, rapping about politics and movies, homoerotic literature, and pasta recipes.

The scene at Ciruela was the best thing to happen to Jonathan in ages: his longtime lover was moving out later that spring, their relationship having fallen into the sort of bland, sexless codependency that characterizes so many long-term affairs, and was taking along with him Bella Abzug, their supersize Maine coon cat. Jonathan would be all alone, after nearly twenty years, left with only empty hangers, stained take-out menus, and memories. Sure, he had been averse to the near-constant changes being made to his beloved "gayborhood," but Jonathan needed a new life, and Ciruela, he surmised, was a welcome respite, one that heralded possibility and the promise of, well, if not love, then certainly lust.

It was at the bar one day that I first came to know Jonathan, when I stopped by on my way home from my writing space to have a glass of wine with Monty. I was deep into a first-draft rewrite of my first book, but that wasn't the reason I found myself spending more and more time at my writing space. No, I did my best to frequently linger away from home—despite having a toddler waiting to see me (and I, her)—because, though I wasn't quite admitting it to myself yet, I simply could not bear to be around my husband. I had become rather expert at avoiding the unavoidable, and when I wasn't burying myself in work, I employed other dodging mechanisms and self-defeating deterrents, like imbibing copious amounts of strong drinks. I wasn't quite at the level of Brick, the alcoholic husband in *Cat on a Hot Tin Roof,* who boozes until he feels "the click" that signifies stupor, but I was finding myself more and more in need of chasing a decent enough buzz to view my world refracted through the benevolence of hooch-colored glasses. The beauty of owning a place like Ciruela was that I could tell myself (and others) that "stopping by" for a glass (or three) of wine was for "practical purposes"; to check in, to see that the operation was running smoothly and that all was hunky-dory. In truth, I was merely killing time (and synapses) before having to face my increasingly hostile "old man."

I don't remember much of what we discussed that first night, Jonathan and I, but I do remember that I found him engaging and intelligent, and that despite his penchant for harangues, he amused me. There was something about him that called to mind various relatives on my father's side: smart, fast-talking, strident—complete with the Catskill-style delivery and quaint Yiddishisms that belied a roiling, unremitting rage. Almost immediately, I learned that, by the time he was eight, Jonathan had been expected to participate in "dinnertime debates," and to do so cogently, no matter the breadth, depth, or maturity of the subject.

This was something I understood all too well as the daughter of an axiom-prone Brooklyn Jew: without fail, one should always have a point of view and be able to present the same with both aplomb and grit. In the absence of subscribing to the more formal aspects of the religion, these sorts of "cultural Jews" insist on their own dogma, making even the most innocuous of topics subject to all the fire of Talmudic dissection. This point was brought home on several occasions over the next few weeks, as I observed Jonathan browbeat any number of young things he hoped to bed with zealous litanies and breathtaking rants. Watching his prey at first try to keep up, then figure "fuck it" before slinking away, it occurred to me that poor Jonathan hadn't a clue how to woo. How could he? What was valued most in his formative years—arguing until you've rendered your opponent / loved one a bloody pulp—was the very genesis of Jonathan's tragic flaw: because the verbal fisticuffs, no matter how impressive, had the paradoxical effect of rendering his insatiable need for human contact all but impossible.

Talk about a boner killer.

Still, there was something about this repellent quality that I found mesmerizing. Like his mentor, the playwright / activist / ACT UP founder Larry Kramer, Jonathan believed it was his moral responsibility to shit-stir, no matter the cost. I often felt like a kid at the movies, eating my popcorn and watching Jonathan take someone to task. It was thrilling to behold, especially because I was not on the receiving end of one of his many wraths.

Over the next few weeks, I began to look forward to our nightly hang at the Ciruela happy hour. Jonathan and I fell into an easy repartee, with me playing a somewhat more intelligent Gracie Allen to his infinitely more bitchy George Burns. I loved how similarly we felt about politicos and celebrities and movies, and he gave me the best recipe for shrimp scampi I've ever had. Our paths crossed at this particular moment in time because we supplied exactly what each of us desired in reverse: Jonathan wished for connection; I, on the other hand, was seeking to disconnect. I didn't want to have to look too terribly deeply at what was making me so unhappy, and spending time with people who genuinely *knew me* would have forced me to do so, or would have pushed the truth to the forefront of my consciousness, at any rate. Making snappy chitchat with a relative stranger as part of barroom bonhomie kept everything I didn't want to deal with at a safe distance. The problem was, as an actress and a people-pleaser, I was awfully good at feigning amity to keep it all going. And Jonathan, by virtue of his neediness, became seduced into believing that he was my new BFF. True, his pushiness might have caused him to glom on and believe we were more bonded than we actually were, despite what I was or wasn't feeding him, but in any other circumstance his presumption would have been nipped in the bud. Instead, its escalation was practically a fait accompli.

"It's so strange," he said one night as we shared a cheese plate and a bottle of rosé. "How is it that I've never met the hubby?"

It *was* strange indeed, but not for the reason to which he was alluding—namely, that Jonathan and I were such "great buds," so how had he not made the acquaintance of my significant other? No, what was unfathomable was how little Sam and I *ever* actually appeared together anymore, how long this had been the case, and the fact that, like the rest of our marital malaise, this reality was being skillfully avoided.

"I'm sure you will soon." I shrugged, then changed the subject.

~

About a week later, sauntering along Eighth Avenue toward Ciruela, I ran into Sam.

"Hey," he said.

"Hey . . ."

We paused, looking at each other, each waiting, I suppose, for the other to carry a conversation that had, by now, grown too heavy to bear. In a few weeks, we would be celebrating our ninth wedding anniversary, though *celebrating* would be a decidedly generous term for what would be more like *tolerating*.

Nine years married, together for almost eleven, and as we stood there in the street, neither of us could muster the energy for even a half smile. I was better at faking it, at least when it came to pleasantries and mundane chats. Sam, on the other hand, was much more present and direct with his gloom, and therefore much more honest. I hated to see him this way, so sad, so spent, so alone. Despite our mostly fractious days and nights, I couldn't help but still feel that it was my role to enliven him, to make him happy, to make him peek out from under the dark cloud that hung over him and revel in the light. I had assumed this role almost from the moment we met in a dark theater lobby in East LA.

It was only later that I would come to feel burdened by this habit, and not long after that, the dark cloud absorbed me, too. I loathed that I had failed in my efforts to infuse his life with joy, and I loathed even more that this failure, which I saw in his eyes each day and eve, eroded my enthusiasm, my spirit, my confidence, and finally, my love. I was his wife, and although his depression predated my existence in his life, I felt it was my job to employ the leaf blower of my life force to blast the dead foliage of his despair away. I suppose I narcissistically thought that I had that kind of power, and the realization that I had nothing of the kind made me not only disconsolate but furious, too. I had failed; our marriage was a mess, but I refused to admit any of it, preferring instead to push on playing hollow scenes with a ghost.

So, with so very much to say, yet lacking the courage to say it, Sam and I once again found ourselves merely grunting monosyllabically at each other, then pausing awkwardly, like characters in a Pinter play, hoping the other would somehow fill the empty spaces, ease the blank stares.

"Some guy named Jonathan is . . . uh . . . ," Sam intoned.

(*Pause.*)

"Oh . . . that guy . . . is he . . . ?" I asked.

"At the bar?"

"Yeah."

"Yeah."

(*Pause.*)

"OK . . . Are you?"

(*Pause.*)

"On my way home?"

"Yeah."

"Yeah."
(*Pause.*)
"OK."
(*Pause.*)
"OK."
(*Pause.*)
"Bye."
"Bye."

He turned to go, and I watched him shuffle along toward our apartment for a minute or two, my eyes fixated all the while on the heels of his shoes, which were horribly worn down. It devastated me to know that their wear was not the result of pounding the cruel city pavement but instead was from the grinding weight of his discontent. I could relate, and moreover, I wished I could Jeannie-blink myself into being his friend again and tell him of my observations. But I wasn't his friend anymore. Now we were in opposite corners, feeling mutually let down and alone. The tenderness we had once shared eluded us, and now, in its place, we were left with this bizarre way of behaving together—like relatives who've survived a terrible catastrophe or life-changing trauma, for whom just seeing each other is too great a reminder of everything that has been frittered away.

When I got to Ciruela, Jonathan was at the bar. I joined him, and Monty set down some olives and two glasses of Argentinian rosé.

"So, I have finally, *finally* met your husband," Jonathan said.

"Yeah?"

"And," he said, popping an olive into his mouth and smile-chewing for a few seconds, "I have just one question."

"OK."

"What are you doing with him?"

I heard this, then thought, *No, I didn't*. Then my mind pressed rewind:

What. Are. You. Doing. With. Him.

And then . . . everything stopped: the conversation, the banter, the fun, the games.

Everything just . . . stopped.

There were a few seconds of weirdness, wherein we both froze, looking at each other in the frisson, somewhat disbelieving we had arrived at the destination to which we had always been hurtling. In the span of those two, maybe three, motionless seconds, Jonathan chuckled a bit, as if he were slightly (but only slightly) embarrassed, while I sat rigid in the repugnance of being caught. But like the many times I'd been in a play and there was a mistake, I recovered quickly, so the scene could carry on. Even though I knew *exactly* what he meant with his not-so-subtle implication, I did the thing where I pretended I was totally clueless. And even though I thought I gave a stellar performance, acting like his innuendo went ten feet over my head, it clearly wasn't good enough for Jonathan, because then he repeated the question.

"What are you doing with him?"

I stared at him with my best level-gazed, Joan Crawford–style, steely fuck-you.

And then I got up and left.

I remember starting to run when I reached the corner. I ran as if I could get away from Jonathan and the truth and everything that had been unlocked in those six words, and, at the same time, I ran toward my husband, as if somehow, by getting to him very quickly, I could stop the bleeding.

I went home, went on with my night, my week, my life, pushing the evening's thorny exchange to the back-est back burner of my mind. But the thing about this awful, totally inappropriate question (that wasn't really a question at all, but a loaded remark about my husband and me) was that it was not something I could easily forget. There was some piece of this rude, obnoxious person's wholly rhetorical "question" that remained with me from that evening on, following me, chasing me, ambushing me when I least expected it. I may have felt at that point mildly or even gravely unhappy, but I didn't really know that we were a couple in trouble.

And, more importantly, I didn't *want* to know.

How could Jonathan, this relative stranger, see what I could not? Moreover, why was it this rando's place to speak up, to presume his position in my life as "tough-love spirit guide" when that had never been granted? Perhaps he felt it necessary, even humane, to shake me out of my complacency. But waking a sleepwalker is dangerous. Not for the sleepwalker, of course, but for the person doing the waking.

Like Anaïs Nin once wrote, "We don't see things as they are, we see them as *we* are." And I was knee-deep in the sort of denial and rote reflexiveness that made seeing anything totally impossible.

And, speaking of seeing, I never saw Jonathan again.

Eleven

The Mourning Dove

I'm not sure when the bird first appeared on the air conditioner outside the living room window, but one Sunday, as June was fading into July, it occurs to me that I've been hearing its plaintive calls for some time. When I finally peer out the window to have a peek, I fully expect to find an owl. Instead, I come upon a brownish-gray bird I assume is a pigeon.

"Can we name her Emily?" the Bear asks.

"Sure," I say, gazing across the courtyard, scanning the other air-conditioning units jutting out of other windows, up and down the red-brick facade, still looking for an owl.

Little Emily, meanwhile, stands there giving me side-eye, and I wonder if she is really the source of the incessant *cooooOOOOO-woo-woo-woo-ing* I am only just realizing I've been hearing for weeks. I take to the Internet, where Google informs me that "Emily" is neither female nor a pigeon—*he* is something called a mourning dove.

Just then, the Bear comes running in to tell me that the witch candle from Enchantments—which I had lit, as per the instructions, the moment I had arrived home five nights before—has finally burned out.

"I didn't even blow it to make a wish, Mama—it just went out," she tells me solemnly as we stand examining the soot-stained glass container that once held my magic candle.

"Maybe Emily blew it out?" the Bear asks.

"No, sweetie," I say, holding her to me and trying to comfort her. "The candle was just finished, that's all."

The Bear scampers off, and I stand there for a second, speculating as to whether or not the candle could have conjured the bird.

Back in my office, I read further:

> When a dove appears it is asking us to go within and release our emotional discord, be it of the past or the present . . . people often find that unexpected and unseen support and assistance comes when they need it most . . . peace will soon be at hand.

From Google's mouth to God's ears.

But what kind of peace? I wonder. Only two evenings before, I had been writing at home, the Bear asleep in her room and Ira in his dog bed beside me, when I heard elated cheers swell in the Chelsea night. Lawmakers had just voted to legalize same-sex marriage in New York, making it the largest state where gay and lesbian couples would be allowed to wed.

Love won, I thought to myself. *Finally.*

And then, as if on cue, Sam walked in with a bouquet of Korean deli roses.

"I want to try," he blurted. "We have so much together. We have . . ." He trailed off, looking at me to help him expand on what those things were, but for once I remained silent. I wanted—or, I suppose, needed—him to do the talking.

"The Bear," he said, finally. "We owe it to her . . ."

I closed my laptop, and we stared at each other for a second or two. Cheers continued to swell outside.

"Are you willing to stop seeing the chick from Miami?" I asked.

"Yes," he said quietly.

I remained seated on the couch; Sam remained standing in front of me, holding the flowers. He had said what we both needed him to say in order for us to proceed, and yet we stayed stuck, frozen in our positions, as if waiting for an unseen stage manager to prompt us as to our next move.

Outside, there was more revelry, then fireworks.

Ira woke from his sleep and began to shake. Sam and I agreed to discuss it all on Monday at our session with Stephen, and with that, he was out the door and back to his sublet.

After soothing Ira, I clipped the Korean deli roses and stuck them into the pottery vase on the dining table, only to realize that I had overclipped the stems, rendering the flowers too short for the vase.

It is an image I cannot shake as I lie in bed the morning of our therapy session—just as I cannot seem to stop picturing Sam standing in front of me, clutching roses wrapped in paper that says "Have good day," his face a mask of distress and, at the same time, exasperation. It was as if he knew the onus to offer the olive branch was on him, but instead of contrite, he felt pissed off. It was not exactly the rapprochement I'd fantasized about. As I drag myself out from under the covers, I once again hear the drawn-out call. Turning to the window, I come face to beak with our feathered squatter. Even though I had told the Bear he was a boy, she still wanted to name him "Emily." His side-eye game is very strong, this Emily. We stare at each other for a few seconds, and as we do, his head bobs back and forth as if trying to peck away the space between us.

> When a dove appears it is asking us to go within
> and release our emotional discord, be it of the past
> or the present . . .

We continue to stare at each other, Emily and I, for another minute or two. Then, turning abruptly to face the rusty brick across the courtyard, he spreads his wings and takes flight.

A few hours later, when I get up to Stephen's room on the third floor, Sam is already there. As I walk across the creaky planks to the overstuffed faux-Navajo sectional, Sam keeps his gaze on the floorboards.

"I'm—I'm just not sure how I feel anymore," Sam says, still looking at the floor. "So much has happened."

I look at Stephen; he looks at me; we look at Sam.

"True," I say. "A lot has happened."

Sam lets out a deep sigh and shakes his head.

"I don't know," he says with a shrug, finally looking at me.

"You don't know what?" I ask.

"How I feel, I guess."

"How you feel about . . . us?"

Sam shrugs.

"About wanting to 'try'?"

He shrugs again.

"I don't know," he says. "I feel . . . different, I guess . . ."

"Different . . . ?"

"Yeah."

"Like . . . ?"

"Like . . . something's changed in me."

There is a pause. Then he says, "I love you, I just don't know if I want to be married to you."

Although only three days before, he came with the Korean deli flowers to say he was ready and willing to work on it, Sam's not entirely sure he wants to be married to me. He's also not entirely sure he wants a divorce (or even an "official" separation). He just keeps repeating that he doesn't know how he feels.

The sense of fury with which I leave the session so staggers me that I walk ten blocks past my apartment, then wonder why the doorman on Thirty-Third Street, who doesn't look at all familiar, stops me from entering.

I meander the outer limits of deepest Chelsea for the next hour, bumping back and forth between housing projects and public gardens, sidewalks and corners, like an unsinkable billiard ball. When I finally make it home, Mark is waiting for me in the lobby. I had blown through the rest of the jewelry money and was once again piling up debt, and Mark suggested we should go through my clothes to see whether he could sell any of them on eBay.

"You look terrible," he says when we get up to my apartment.

"Thanks."

"What's going on now?"

I tell him about the roses and what happened at Stephen's and that, as a result, my psyche has pole-vaulted back into the headspace of "if only I could sufficiently change myself, Sam would recommit to me and us and everything would be hunky-dory," a position that frustrates Mark to no end.

"Ugh," he says, rolling his eyes as we sort through clothes and shoes. "Again with this?"

"Listen—I brought something to this picnic, and it wasn't just potato salad."

"Honey, look: Are there some things you could learn about yourself? Sure. And it'll be something to look forward to when you've ended this marriage, because, Nance . . . you need to end this marriage—you do. And you need to do that first, before trying to figure out your part in what happened."

Mark gasps, then holds up a rather unfortunate pair of faux-python loafers.

"When were you a lesbian who worked at a bank?"

"I've made some very bad decisions in my life, obviously."

"Nothing that can't be fixed," he says, tossing the loafers into the eBay pile.

"Maybe it's cuz of my gig writing for Paul, but I keep trying to think of pop songs that align thematically with my situation. Sorta helps me, I guess, in thinking about it all. Today, all day, it's been the Monkees' 'A Little Bit Me, a Little Bit You' . . ."

Mark nods. No one gets this more than Mark.

"I think it's great that you can be so expansive and generous and can embrace the attitude that it takes two people to make or break a relationship. I admire that, I really do," he says thoughtfully. "That said, in terms of 'A Little Bit Me, a Little Bit You,' I'd argue that it's 'A Little Bit You, but Mostly It's Him.'"

"That's only because you love me," I say.

"It's true," he says, holding my hand. "I do. And you know what song I'd pick for you?"

"Is it Barbra?"

"Of course."

"Which?"

"'Enough Is Enough.' Cuz, Nance?"

"Yeah?"

"It is."

~

That evening, I attend a play in the Village. The play, an existential riff on the banalities of television, is beyond redemption. As I watch, I am struck by how much actors are willing to brave just so they can say "I am in a play—I am working." Like abused children, no matter how awful the material, they seem impervious to what they endure and don't seem to understand why anyone having to bear witness might find it at all disturbing. I can relate, and not just because I spent many years as an actor. When I am not fantasizing about killing the playwright and director, my thoughts turn to the starring role I play in the charade that is my own life. As is true for the players currently strutting and fretting their hour upon the stage, rational thought has been supplanted by a mentality best known to junkies: "Just one more and then I'm done."

Just one more week, and then I'll tell Sam it's over; just one more transfusion, and then I'll put Ira to sleep.

But the moment my magical thinking bestows even the tiniest shred of a kinda-sorta reason to hold on, keep going, put off, delay, I breathe a sigh of relief that, today, nothing will end. Today, everything is, if not OK, then at least the same, allowing me to revel, once more, in the deceptively calming waters of stasis.

A scene comes to mind, from a few days before, when I took Ira to see Jim. He knew the point I was at; he knew I couldn't stop—not yet. And he wanted to offer no judgments, only to do his job. We had one of those conversations I find reminiscent of a drama school acting exercise wherein the objective is to intuit what's *really* going on with the other person. Short dialogues, no superfluous words, a delivery that is careful and weighted, über-consciously making sure you hear your scene partner's response, making equally sure you have been heard:

JIM: He's not doing well today.

ME: I know. Can we—

JIM: Transfuse?

ME: Yes.

JIM: We can—

ME: Unless you think—

JIM: No—we can.

ME: OK.

(*Pause.*)

ME: You don't think he's—

JIM: He's . . . ?

ME: Going to die?

JIM: You mean right now?

ME: Yes.

JIM: No.

ME: OK.

JIM: It's just that . . . it's all so experimental, and I don't want you to—

ME: I know.

JIM: And you're spending a lot of money, so—

ME: I know, but—

(*Pause.*)

JIM: OK.

ME: I know there are no guarantees, but . . .

JIM: No.

ME: I just feel like . . . I have to try.

JIM: OK.

ME: Thank you.

JIM: We'll take it from here.

I think about the blood I am pumping into my dog, and I am awash with feelings of self-reproach for making him stay alive simply because I am going through the absolute worst time in my life and am too terrified to feel my way through the multitude of concurrent loss. How long can this continue? When does one know, as Barbra sang, that "enough is enough"? I think of Sam and his wavering, and though his ambivalence in the past has infuriated me, now I feel only empathy. After all, he is not the only one stuck. Like my husband, I, too, am unable to move forward. So, instead, I move laterally, wrapped in a shroud of half-truths, equivocating, even to myself, about how grim the situation really is, yet at the same time, trying to move through my days with purpose and with a solid plan.

I consider the fact that, in Ira's case, anyway, it all began with kidney failure—the failure to rid the system of toxins. I wonder how such a condition even begins. Where does the fault lie? Was it predestined? Was this his fate? Was he born with a particular structural weakness that, no matter what, would out itself over time? Or was it something that could have been contained had it been caught in time? If so, when had been the turning point? When had the toxins gotten so numerous, so out of control, that they became impossible to manage?

The actors on stage continue to bravely march on through the tangle of words meant to titillate and shock. They betray no hint of humiliation—that is for the audience to do on their behalf. As one scene shifts aimlessly to the next, it dawns on me that, in my own drama, I am both the player and the audience: I do what is necessary to perpetuate the plot, and at the very same time, I am the horrified onlooker suppressing my screams.

Audience members begin to leave in a steady stream, and yet I stay still, immobilized in my seat. During the many interminable on-stage silences, the uptown A train can be heard rumbling by. Here we are, those of us daring or stupid enough to stay, while life, meanwhile, continues outside the theater. The wheels turn no matter what we wish; we are not behind those particular controls. Aside from the incessant roar of the subway, another sound emerges. At first, I think I'm imagining it, but then I hear it again and again, the sound getting stronger and more fervent.

CooooOOOOO-woo-woo-woo.

There is a moment that I think it's Emily, the mourning dove—my mourning dove—and that he's followed me. But no matter how screwed up I am, I know this could not be possible. Perhaps the mourning sound is not coming from outside but is instead something internal, something that shadows me now no matter how far I get from home. Something else troubles me as I sit in the darkened theater, something even more sinister, more foreboding, and that is the sense that, even though I sit in the last row with no one else around me, I am not alone. I feel the energy that has sidled up to the empty seat beside me, and

I understand immediately that this is not a person but a thing called Grief. Like a masher trying to put the moves on, Grief inches closer and closer, and though I am terribly intimidated, I lie low, hold my breath, and continue to look straight ahead. The thing is, though, I know that none of this matters—I have finally been caught, and Grief, like the sound of the mourning dove, will continue to stalk me wherever I go. Because, no matter how clever my hiding space, from now on, I will always be in plain sight.

JULY

Twelve

INDEPENDENCE DAY

The Evite has an image of a giant wine bottle exploding in a Jackson Pollock-y splatter, and aside from the date and time, it bears three words: *Sexy Summer Bash*.

It is to be held at some swanky country club in Bridgehampton, hosted jointly by two couples, exceedingly nice people, who had been some of Ciruela's most devoted regulars. I am not especially in a party headspace. In fact, it would be totally understandable, given what's going on in my life, to see something like this thing in my inbox, say to myself, *Sounds fun, but my marriage is in the shitter, so I'll give this a skip*, hit "Delete," and carry on with the regularly scheduled rending of garments.

But I don't do that.

Instead, I see this invitation, immediately dispense with any of the tricky particulars of my current life, don the rosiest-colored glasses in the history of rose-colored glasses, and with all the conviction in the world, say to myself, *What could be more perfect than going to this Gatsbyesque occasion on Long Island, where, under the summer stars and cooled by the ocean breezes, my husband and I will dance together while sharing lingering kisses, before returning to our hotel room to make love? What could possibly be more delicious or divine—or exactly what we need right here and right now—than this Sexy Summer Bash Thingy, during which we will laugh, love, eat, drink, and be whatever is merrier than merry?* And it won't even have to end *there*, because the Sexy Summer Bash Thingy and the sexy sex we have *after* the Sexy Summer Bash Thingy will then cross-fade into a lovely morning, wherein we wend our way to, I don't know, let's say Amagansett (because I love Amagansett, I really do; I even love *saying* Amagansett, that's how much I love Amagansett). Maybe we take a beautiful drive around Amagansett; maybe we drive around Amagansett, looking for the weatherworn farmhouse Arthur Miller and Marilyn Monroe lived in during the happiest part of their marriage, when Arthur was writing the novella that became *The Misfits* and Marilyn, off the various pills and booze and whatever else she usually needed to swallow to keep her prodigious demons at bay, was trying to get pregnant. And even if we don't find the happy home where Marilyn and Arthur spent two relatively idyllic summers in Amagansett, we won't be too terribly bummed, because, *for god's sake, we are in Amagansett*, which in and of itself is enough to make our hearts sing—and because Amagansett is home to the famous Lobster Roll, which we of course have to hit, so we can sit at those little lopsided tables along Montauk Highway, munching on fried clams and sweet corn and crinkle fries and the best lobster rolls ever, before leisurely driving back to the city, relaxed, refreshed, and more in love than ever before . . .

If there is a signpost signaling Danger! Delusional barely married currently on slalom course, hurtling toward cement wall she thinks is a field of peonies, I don't see it. If there is even a solitary peep of a quiet but nevertheless vehement inner voice saying, *I think we might need to check you into the bin, bitch, cuz you cray,* I don't hear it.

And I won't see or hear anything until later, when, stopping by the wine shop, I share the invitation with Sam.

"I thought this seemed fun," I say.

"How much will it cost us?" he asks.

I am initially flummoxed by his retort. *Cost* us? Does Sam honestly think this swank affair has an admission fee? Because, for the life of me, I cannot recall ever before having been charged to go to a social gathering, save for keg parties in high school. It's a nice invitation, from nice people, to attend a nice party. It seems to me a nice idea. But that's just it—it's an idea, *my* idea, *my* fantasy, one that is totally unrealistic. And it is this that is the very nature of Sam's concern: Here we are, neither here nor really even there, in limbo, still unclear. And here *I am*, asking, yet again, for something—another "expenditure" that will undoubtedly make Sam feel pressured and uncomfortable. *He isn't wrong*, I think, when he expands on his initial consternation: taking this trip, or any trip, to Bridgehampton would mean getting a rental car, a hotel, a babysitter, a dog sitter, etc. It would mean money shelled out for gas and food and whatever else we'd need to take a two-day trip to the beach. With our financials in such a shambles, how could we, Sam wants to know, possibly entertain the notion of "extras"? I can envision myself in the past, giving voice to the philosophy that some things are about more than the practical, that to weigh each proffer on the basis of cost is to know the price of everything and the value of nothing. But in this instance, I find myself not getting defensive or angry or even focusing on the usual ways in which Sam and I disappoint each other. Instead, I am overcome by sadness. How did we get so very far away— from each other, from how we used to be, from Amagansett, and from the shared imagination that might conjure such a trip?

That night, unable to sleep, I lie staring up at the potted ficus tree that stands over our bed. I had this idea, when we were putting together our boudoir, that it might be fun to sleep beneath a tree, so I found one in the Flower District and hauled it home in a grocery cart. I'm not good with plants; in fact, I have a real brown thumb, killing any and every plant with which I come into contact. This is not because I neglect them; rather, it is because I am too much. Striving to love them with all that I am, I end up overwatering and ultimately drowning any and all flora with the very thing that should provide them sustenance. Sam, on the other hand? Plants are his domain. All plant life thrives when he's in the vicinity—like Bruce, the Charlie Brown Christmas tree he rescued from the trash when we first met. But our tree, even with Sam as caretaker, never thrived. At best, one side grew leaves while the other was brittle and close to barren, as if it couldn't make up its mind whether to live or die. "This isn't the right environment for it," Sam always maintained. "We should give it away to someone whose space has more light." But I couldn't give it up. And who was I serving with this refusal? Certainly not the tree. But I know now that Sam is right: if the tree has a chance, it will be with someone else. But as I lie staring up at the branches, I allow myself the briefest of moments to fathom a room with an abundance of light, where everything in it blooms, and a universe in which neither Sam nor I is to blame for not turning out to be what the other really wanted.

Even though it is a million o'clock, I call Stephen. I know I will only get his machine, but like any middle-of-the-night inspiration, I know it must be recorded immediately, lest it be consigned to oblivion. I tell him I need to come in ASAP—alone—and to please let me know his availability. By the time I wake up in the morning, I have an email:

> I have a cancellation for this morning—can you come in at 9?

~

Sometime after the appointed time, I am sitting on Stephen's couch, which feels suddenly quite large, as if it grew several sizes since last I found myself seated upon it. It's the same, of course; I, on the other hand, am not. And I'm also alone. Both of these things make me feel incredibly small, like Cindy Lou Who, the tiniest of the tiny Whos of Whoville.

Stephen and I talk about how giving Sam space and time to work through his existential crisis, along with the haze of all the back and forth, has become too toxic for me. I express concern about the Bear, who is obviously being deeply affected by the tension and hostility that, whether we want it to or not, roils beneath the surface of our every interaction.

"She asked me, 'Why does Dad act like he hates you?' the other day, which of course just killed me," I tell Stephen, pausing to root around in my pocket for a tissue to soak up the river of tears my face has become. "It just killed me."

Stephen nods, then swivels in his chair to grab the tissue box off his desk.

"Here," he says, gingerly pushing it toward me on the table between his shrink chair and the couch. "Just breathe . . . just breathe and let go. You've been holding a lot. And I'm sure I don't have to tell you this, but Sam doesn't hate you—"

"I know," I say. "Only my essence."

Stephen laughs softly, shaking his head.

"It's true—he really does."

"I think the truth is that you're not even 'you'—you're a projection."

"Meaning what?"

"Meaning that you're not real to him right now. You've become a projection, and unless and until, as I've pointed out before, we are willing to work with our own projections, it's impossible to ferret out what's what and who's who."

"I'm willing to work with my projections," I say.

"I know."

There is a pause, during which I momentarily feel light-headed and lose my place in the conversation. When I finally get my bearings, I ask Stephen the question I have been wanting to ask, yet avoiding, for the better part of the last year:

"How do you know when it's over?"

"I think you have to ask yourself what you can tolerate," he says. "And for how long. Everyone's threshold for pain is different."

"I don't know how to do this. I don't know how to quit."

"Can you surrender?"

"That's what I mean—I feel like I just . . . like I'm not ready to . . . give up."

"Surrender's not about giving up—it's about giving *over*. It's about letting go of illusions and the attachment to a particular outcome, and making space for what's happening right now, inside us and around us. Because the moment we open to it, the moment we make that space, that's when we start to really change; that's when we begin to learn and grow."

I think about what Stephen's saying for a moment. I hear him, and I get it. I know he's right. But there are still so many blocks. I can't seem to get myself into the end zone.

"I know," I say. "I just thought we'd do it together. I really did—I thought that the crisis itself would, I don't know, shock us both into really wanting to make it work. And maybe that happened—maybe we both did, really did, want to make it work, and we just . . . couldn't. I really thought I'd figure it out, you know? Surrender feels so pathetic and weak."

"Well, that's where you're wrong, Nancy. Because *surrendering* is not an act of weakness; it's a feat of courage."

"What would it even look like? What happens when someone 'surrenders'?"

"Well, what happens is one or both of you arrives at some sort of mindful acceptance of what is. And then someone has to be the brave one. Someone has to be brave enough to say to the other, 'I see you—I see that you're unhappy. I see *you* as unhappy as *I* am. I see our daughter as unhappy. I see *all of us* only growing unhappier each day. And I have to believe there's a future version of us in which we find the happiness we all deserve. Perhaps that happiness is to be found with other partners or within ourselves, by ourselves. But I believe in your potential for happiness, as I believe in my own.' It comes down to one of you having to be brave enough for both of you to believe that stepping forward into the realm of 'not knowing' is for the greatest good of everyone involved. That takes courage. Courage and faith."

Faith. *The unequivocal faith one must have to venture forth in darkness,* the rabbi said on our wedding day.

Stephen leans forward and looks me very intently in the eye.

"I think you are a person of great courage, Nancy."

"Are you saying I should be the one to end it?"

"I'm saying that it would be understandable for you to say to yourself, 'I can't do this anymore; it's too painful for me to continue,'" Stephen says slowly. "And that I would support you in arriving at that place."

"He saved my life, you know."

"Sam?"

"Yes. When we were first dating, my car broke down on the Santa Monica Freeway, and I called him, and he just raced over and . . . I don't even know how the fuck he found me, but . . . he plucked me out of my car in the middle of the freeway and . . . saved me."

Stephen smiles. "Such gallantry."

"You know what?"

"What?"

"I've failed at everything that ever meant anything to me."

"I don't believe that."

"I have."

"Look—it's not about failing or achieving. It's about just being. Being human. Humans, being. And you know something, that doesn't preclude change—it actually empowers it."

"Whatever. Sorry. I know—I'm being all Gen-X-y cynical and shit. It's just like . . . *why*? You know? Why did I go through all this? All the crazy-ass shit I've done. What was the point?"

"Because you had to. You needed to. There are no shortcuts to wisdom. You know that T. S. Eliot poem 'Little Gidding'?"

I shake my head.

"'We shall not cease from exploration / And the end of all our exploring / Will be to arrive where we started / And know the place for the first time.'"

"Hmm. Not sure I get it."

"You've been on a pretty intense adventure this year. You couldn't know anything before the adventure, and you also couldn't know anything, or enough, let's say, in the midst of your exploration. But once you get home, when your journey comes to an end, you'll see everything you couldn't see before—including yourself. And, I guess, to answer your question, that's the point of all the crazy shit *any of us* do, you know?"

"Is it totally fucked up that I'm still holding out hope that when . . ." I start crying again—I can barely get the words out.

"That when . . . ?" Stephen asks, leaning forward and tilting his head.

"That when Ira . . . dies . . . Is it totally fucked up that I still hold out hope that his . . . passing will bring us back together?"

Stephen smiles. "No," he says. "Not fucked up at all. Believe in yourself, Nancy. And remember: you're not surrendering to the opposition, but to your own resistance. And when you're able to do that, well, that's when you're truly free."

I see us then, Sam and me, all those years ago on that chaotic strip of freeway, him screaming, me jumping, us driving, my jalopy getting smaller and smaller in the distance. I'd always wanted to return the favor—to save Sam.

Now maybe I had a chance.

〜

Later that day, Ira and I are at the vet. It is just before Fourth of July weekend, exactly one year from the time that the renal failure was first diagnosed. Ira seems especially chipper: tail waggy, ears up, appetite full—my boy. Our visit today is fairly routine; we are just there to do weekly blood work, check iron levels, etc., and though we have been waiting a strangely long time, I am untroubled, figuring that, with the holiday weekend looming, they are especially busy. Ira is panting and smiling, has his tongue out and front paws, as usual, wrapped around my neck.

"In a few weeks," I tell him, "you'll be twelve. You made it, doggy. We made it."

Just then, Jim's associate, Gabby, comes into the examination room to explain the delay. Apparently, Ira's red blood cells are at an all-time low.

"His PCV is at ten," she tells me, referring to the term for measuring the packed cell volume. A normal value for dogs is anywhere between thirty-five and fifty-seven, and while Ira's has been low, it hasn't been this low in a year. In fact, remarkably, the last time it was this low was Fourth of July weekend exactly one year ago. But how could that be? I know what a "ten" looked like—it looked like he was at death's door—and this was not a dog at "ten." At least, not outwardly. I am in complete shock, and so is Gabby.

"It makes no sense," Gabby says, shrugging sadly. "That's why it was taking so long; I made them run it again because I just couldn't believe it." Her eyes fill with tears. "I'm so sorry."

Gabby leaves to find Jim and apprise him. When he comes in a few moments later, he doesn't mince words. "Pretty soon, you're going to have to . . . make a decision."

"You mean—"

Jim nods.

"Now?"

Jim sighs. "Think about it. Do you want to call your husband?"

"The thing is . . . I'm . . . actually not sure I really have a husband at this point."

And that's when I lose it. Total blubbering mess. Ira, despite his apparent dire straits, maintains a hearty appreciation for my snot, lapping up the torrents just as soon as they stream out of my nose.

"I'm so sorry," Jim says. "I had no idea."

"Things have been so bad," I squeak, continuing to sob uncontrollably. "But I'm still hopeful that we'll—"

Jim nods, rubbing my shoulder.

"I'm not sure we're . . . it's over, but . . . I have to . . . make a decision . . ."

"I'm so sorry," he says again. "I knew you didn't want him to know about the bills, but I didn't think . . . it's hard to ever really know what's going on with people, you know?"

"Yeah . . ."

Jim sighs. "All this stuff is hard. Life is hard. End of life is hard."

We stroke Ira as we talk, and I still cannot believe that the dog who stands wagging his tail gaily, as if the conversation were about a day trip to the beach, is actually dying. I should know this at this point, and yet it is as impossible to fathom as it was the moment I first heard he was sick.

"What always trips me up is I kept wanting to know from him that he's done, you know? A sign, a signal, something that lets me know he's ready to go. But then he's like . . . this. Waggy tail, chipper. Smiling. He smiles, you know."

"Oh, I know."

"You do?"

"I do."

"I hate when people don't think dogs smile. Cuz they do. They really do."

Jim nods and smiles. "Oh, Ira," he says, rubbing his head.

"Why does he seem so happy? I mean, why, if he's so sick, does he seem so . . ." I can barely choke out the word again. "Happy . . . ?" I say before dissolving once more.

"Because he's a beagle," Jim says, smiling. "Beagles are always happy, even when they're not."

There is a pause.

"But I also think it's possible that he knows you're not in a good place. And he loves you. You're the love of his life."

"I am?"

Jim nods. "Of course. And he wants to know that you're gonna be OK. I really believe that. They need to feel at peace—that their people are at peace."

The love of his life. I had never been "the love of someone's life," and it had always been something that bothered me. People had loved me—Sam, others—but as deep as their feelings had been, I had certainly never been described in that way. Love of his life. *How unfair,* I think, *that the one time I'm actually considered the love of someone's life, I'm only really getting to grasp it when the life in question is just about over.*

We stand there for a few moments, Jim rubbing my shoulder as I continue to weep, and petting Ira as he continues to lick my salty secretions.

"Look," Jim says. "You still have two more infusions left. I mean, you paid for them already, they're here, and they're yours. Let's do one today, get him stable and comfortable, and see where we are after the weekend."

Jim leaves to prepare for the transfusion, leaving Ira and me alone in the examination room. In his absence, I search the eyes of the one being, aside from my child, who has never abandoned me, looking for a clue as to how I should proceed, what he'd like me to do.

"What do you think, doggy, huh? We don't have to do this anymore, doggy, you know? I can still tell him we're done if you want."

I think about how he has been more of a partner to me than my human partner, more of a friend than any of my friends, more my fantasy version of a "family member" than anyone I'm blood-related to. *What,* I think to myself, *have I ever given him? What have I done for him, aside from selfishly prolong his life for my own benefit?*

185

"I haven't deserved you, doggy," I say. "I want you to know, though, that you can go. You can go, and you don't need to worry. I don't want to keep . . . keeping you. Next time you don't feel well—whenever it is—I will help you. Jim will come over. We will do it at home, on Mommy's bed. We will play Dolly Parton."

~

It is the Fourth of July. Sam and I have taken the Bear to a garden party in Chelsea, then to the roof of London Terrace to watch the fireworks show. The Bear is cranky and tired, and there are too many people on the roof on this muggy evening, so we leave before the fireworks even begin. I am exhausted. I have never been this tired. Maybe it's the heat; maybe it's the cumulative effect of the past few days. Maybe it's both.

I lie down on the bed. Sam tucks the Bear in, after which he joins me, lying on the bed. The fireworks begin. I am facing away from him; he is holding me from behind, our bodies intertwined like the braided *havdalah* candle we lit when we observed Shabbat in the early years of our marriage. *Havdalah* . . . the Hebrew word for separation. It is a ceremony that begins on Saturday evening upon the appearance of three stars in the sky, symbolizing the distinction between the previous week and the next, between the light and the dark, the spiritual and the mundane. Beautiful, bittersweet, it reminds us that, while the dreamlike time of Shabbat is over, there is hope that its sweetness will follow us into the dawn of a new beginning.

I am reminded of this ritual, the one with the candle, as I consider the one in which we are currently engaged, wherein, as if by some mutual wordless consent, we lie wrapped up, enmeshed, like the candle, with no visible beginning or end.

Sam's right arm is around me, and we are clasping hands; I keep trying to imagine that it is not now, but a long time ago, when we were in the first blushes of love, only I can't seem to accomplish this feat of mental gymnastics.

Were we ever really like this?

I know we were affectionate and tender and deeply in love once, and yet it all seems so implausible, so fantastical, as though I am bearing witness to someone else's dream. This is never more true than when Sam, attempting to define this gauzy moment, says that he understands it as "a new form of contact," one that indicates that we have been "liberated from past bondage." I hear his words and marvel at how differently I perceive what is transpiring, how, to me, this moment does not augur a rosy future but instead serves as a kind of desperate plea to return to a gilded past. In my mind, I see us like survivors of a sunken ship, clinging less to each other than to the wreckage of our marriage, clutching the last vestiges of its pieces, in the hopes of being saved. Sam and I, it seems, have swapped places. He—holding fast to the premise that we still, as his anniversary card to me had said, have so very much to celebrate—is in his own version of Amagansett; I, on the other hand, see nothing other than the painful paradox of our woven-together bodies, closer than ever yet drifting further and further apart. "You're not surrendering to the opposition but to your own resistance," Stephen had said. "And when you're able to do that, well, that's when you're truly free."

Fireworks are exploding in a crescendo over the Hudson River; we are into the finale of the celebration of our country winning its independence. The sky is flooded by occasional glints of light that reflect off the red brick of the interior courtyard. The river isn't visible from where I lie frozen on the bed, wrapped up in the arms of the man I will tell in four days that our marriage is over, but I keep imagining I can see them anyway. I think of those red curlicues and ecstatic bursts, and those rebels and their bloody battle to win sovereignty. Did it ever occur to them that freedom was a tad overrated?

Just then, the fireworks come to an abrupt end.

The celebration is over. And so are we.

Thirteen

DINOSAURS DIVORCE

On a stunningly beautiful Saturday in July, fourteen years and one day exactly from the night we met in an East Los Angeles theater, Sam comes over at noon so that we can tell our six-year-old that life as she knows it will never be the same. We stand together, barely breathing, in the kitchen, while the Bear sits on the leopard couch and watches the end of *The Fresh Beat Band*, a Nickelodeon show about a merry band of coeds who use their songs to solve problems.

"We had a great day," the Fresh Beat Band sings. *"The very best day / And nothing could be better . . ."*

I want the Fresh Beat Band to do a show in which they puzzle out how parents can announce their split without anyone being the slightest bit upset, I think, as Sam and I wait anxiously in the wings, ready to drop the bomb our precious child has no idea is coming. But by the time we crawl out to take our places beside her on the couch and begin our rehearsed speech, the Bear, anticipating this very episode, has a script that is entirely her own. We are not able to get more than a few pathetic psycho-babbly words out before she jumps off the couch, covers her ears, and starts screaming:

"Nooooooooooo!! Nooooooooooo!! Nooooooooooo!!"

With that, she marches into her room to begin packing.

"I am moving out of here!" she screams repeatedly, throwing shit all over the bedroom, noisily opening and then slamming drawers and closet doors and hurling books and dolls and anything else she can get her hands on. Ira comes to sit by us, next to the couch, cowering in fear as the Bear continues to rue the day she ever met any of us.

"Well," I say to Sam. "That went well."

After about an hour, we are able to calm the Bear. We convince her that the three of us should go to the water park for ice cream. It is a perfect summer day. We make our way over to the water park, the Bear riding on Sam's shoulders, and I sauntering beside them. We are almost like every one of the happy families we see frolicking on grass so green it looks like a movie set. We stay for a long time—too long, in fact—because when we have to leave, the spell is broken, and the Bear, realizing that the dream was not the miserable part in our apartment, but the fun-filled two-ice-cream-cone after-party, begins, once again, to scream and cry.

Later that night, while giving her a bath, I read *Dinosaurs Divorce*, a children's book in which kindly, anthropomorphized cartoon dinosaur children deal with the end of their parents' marriage. After I towel her off, we sit on the edge of the tub and read it through together slowly, one more time.

"What About You?" the book asks in a heading. "When your parents divorce, it's natural to feel . . ." followed by eight colorfully illustrated frames, in which kid dinosaurs demonstrate their feelings: sad, angry, afraid, confused, etc.

"Can you find your dinosaur?" I ask the Bear. "Is there a dinosaur in any of these pictures that's like how *you* feel?"

She shrugs and shakes her head.

"Sad . . . confused . . . ?" I ask.

The Bear nods.

"Which one, sweetie?"

"Angry!" she shouts. *"An-gry, an-gry!!"* she shouts again and again, before collapsing onto the black-and-white bathroom floor tile in bitter tears.

I scoop her up to hold and soothe her, and as she leans against me, she wails uncontrollably, repeating over and over her intent to move in with our downstairs neighbor.

"I don't care if Susie's apartment is messy. I am moving in with her—and you and Dad can't stop me!"

I put the toilet seat down, sit on it, and pull her onto my lap, and we stay there, both of us crying, rocking back and forth for a long time.

"I wish there was a dinosaur book for you, Mama," she tells me as I tuck her in later. "We need to find a dinosaur for your feelings, too."

"Mommy's gonna be OK, sweetie," I tell her, doing my damnedest to inhabit my new role as "plucky single mom." "You don't have to worry—Mommy's a grown-up and can take care of herself, and she can take care of you, too. And same with Dad. We're all gonna be fine. I know it hurts, and it's sad, and it wasn't what we wanted, but someday soon, sweetie, I promise, we're all gonna be . . ."

"Back together?" the Bear squeaks, in the tiniest voice I've ever heard.

"Happy," I tell her. "Someday soon, we will all be happy."

I'm not sure she's buying it, because let's face it, it isn't exactly an Ellen Burstyn in *Alice Doesn't Live Here Anymore*, Oscar-level performance, but given the fact that it all went down only a few hours before, it's the best I can do.

It takes longer than usual, but when she finally falls asleep, I sneak back into the bathroom with a big glass of wine, and for the first time in seven years, I light a cigarette. It's been eons, but it's as if we never said goodbye, cigarettes and me. I light some incense and a couple of scented candles, and straddling the toilet, I blow smoke out the window into the perfect summer night. Though it is dark, all of Manhattan is enveloped in a glorious indigo color. I think of those couples out on Long Island, sun-dappled, laughing, a little buzzed, cooled by the ocean breezes, dancing under the stars at that Gatsbyesque Sexy Summer Bash. I can hear them from my perch, enjoying each other in ways Sam and I never would. I'm not jealous, exactly, just sad and spent, relieved somewhat by the end of amorphousness, and hopeful that one day we will all be, as I assured the Bear, happy. Exhaling into the indigo night, I strain to imagine the future version of myself, the unmarried woman version, the "divorcée."

Divorcée.

I remember hearing that word for the first time when I was a kid. One of my mother's friends was considering getting her real estate license.

"But then I realized," she told my mother, "that it was a job for a *divorcée* . . ."

I remember the way she emphasized the word *divorcée*, as if it were comparable to *whore* or *tainted, irredeemable woman*, and the way my mother looked at her when she said it, as if there could be no fate worse.

As antiquated as that might sound, I will find out that some of the more quaint notions of a divorced woman will remain, no matter what century we currently inhabit. And, much to my chagrin, I will learn about it first and foremost from the Yummy Mummies. After my marriage ends, I will see the Yummy Mummies only one final time, when they take me out to dinner to be debriefed about the demise of my marriage. There will be drinks and hugs and delicious French fries and chocolate and more drinks, during which I will feel consoled, supported, and adored beyond measure. I will leave this evening feeling that, no matter what, the Yummy Mummies have my back—never, not for one second, will I have to "wait to exhale" without my posse of forever "mom friends."

And I will feel this way until one day when I come across pictures on Facebook of a Yummy Mummy dinner to which I had not been invited. I will initially not take it to heart—that is, until I see another.

And another. And then after the third time, it will dawn on me: I have been excommunicated. I will initially feel an array of things: pissed off, hurt, miffed by what, to me, was an egregious exclusion. I will thereupon make it my mission to refuse to "like" any of their future posts, cross-posts, pictures, and tags—as if my absurd little rubber sword were any genuine match for the Uzi of perceived rejection that festered within the petulant vessel of defeat I had become.

Can it be? I will marvel as I torture myself by taking a lurking tour of the disco parties, barbecues, birthdays, random dinners, and other swell soirees, only acceptable if attached to a man, a husband—*Did they, in fact, side with Sam? Or had my emotional spillage, as I made my way through the stages of coming to grips with my new normal, been so unseemly and obnoxious that they collectively were all just like, "I can't"? Or were there other, more sinister, far-reaching implications? Was being a (gasp) divorcée synonymous with being a wanton hussy, and they had to batten down their marital hatches lest I lure their husbands away with my wicked vacu-vadge?* At some point, however, my indignation will dissipate. I will realize that the more probable scenario was likely much more unconscious on their part, and that my being given the bum's rush was the natural result of something with which I could truly empathize: profound fear.

Maybe like with copycat suicide, marital demise in close proximity was something that was in danger of being emulated, or, worse, like a devastating plague that could be caught.

Or maybe it was even simpler: that being around me was like being visited by the Ghost of Christmas Yet to Come, the most fearsome of all spirits, whose chilling mask of vague horrors is emblematic of all that could and might very well go wrong.

I stub out my cig on the outer edge of the sill and drop the butt into the toilet. I don't flush; I'm about to light another and want to wait until I'm finished with that one—or the next one, or the next one after that—before making any noise that might awaken the Bear. I sidle over to the medicine cabinet, and after briefly peering at my silhouetted image in the chipped mirror, I open the door and reach for the Xanax. Wine is not nearly enough to quell the around-the-clock spin class that has been cycling through my insides for the past few days. I swallow two, then move back to my very glamorous spot straddling the can and fire up another smoke. Inhaling my long-lost friend as if it were my very life force, the bitter burn of benzos at the back of my tongue, I resolve to take my life going forward not "one day at a time" but, instead, one cigarette at a time.

I am exhausted—from the day, the wine, the Xanax. I toss the remains of my cig into the toilet, sit down on the edge of the tub, and pick up the dinosaur book. In the candlelight, I flip through the pages, marveling at what a dowdy, blowsy bunch these dinosaur moms are. It would be nice to have a dinosaur book I could relate to, as the Bear suggested, something that, if it couldn't speak to the specifics of my situation, at least resembled me. And just as soon as that thought enters my mind, I see her: Flip Wilson as Geraldine—reddish wig, swigging martinis, "dino-wino," and popping pills—troubled, yes, but still, she is pretty fucking great.

And though it has been arguably the shittiest day of my life, at least I've found my dinosaur.

Fourteen

WHEN DINOSAURS DIE

It is six in the morning, on a Sunday, three days before Ira's twelfth birthday, when in my semi-sleep I hear a howl, a yelp, and then the sound of frantic scratching. I jump out of bed and run, to find Ira lying on the floor in the hallway, and though he's on his side, he's running like a bat out of hell. I remember my grandmother's dog, Misty, a black lab afflicted all his life with epilepsy. Every now and then, Misty would hit the deck and look just like this. The running goes on for about thirty seconds, after which Ira's body stiffens and his jaw clenches.

A seizure, I think to myself, *Ira's having a seizure.*

When the seizing stops, I pull him into my embrace. I'm not sure whose heart it is I feel thumping—Ira's or mine. When I pull back slightly, I look into his face. I can tell that he's blind. I am utterly terrified, and though it is 6:45 a.m. on a Sunday, I call Jim on his cell phone. "Grand mal seizure," he tells me. Because it's Sunday, not only is Jim's office closed, but he's in the country and he won't be returning until six in the evening.

"I can't do it to him anymore," I tell him. "It's time. I have to do it today."

Jim tells me I have two choices: I can take Ira to the emergency hospital and have him put to sleep there, or if I'm willing to wait, he'll come directly to my apartment when he gets back, and we can do it here. I choose the latter; we've come this far, and I hate the idea of bringing him to a cold hospital, where he doesn't know anyone and would be frightened. I've been thinking about this moment for a year: I want him to be at home, surrounded by the things he knows—even if he can't see them anymore, he can at least smell them and hear them. The catch is, of course, we must wait. I look at the clock. It's just after seven a.m. Eleven hours. We have eleven hours left.

Sam comes to take the Bear to breakfast and then to drop her off with her friend from upstairs, Stella, and Stella's two moms. This had been prearranged because, as it happens, I have a Shaffer script due in the morning and had planned to spend the day writing punch lines.

"Whatsa matter with Ira, Mama?" the Bear asks before leaving with Sam.

"He's not doing very well, sweetie."

"Is he dying?"

"Yes."

"Is he dying right now?"

"No—the doctor has to come over first."

"And then he'll die?"

"Yes."

"Can I be here?"

"If you want to, yes."

"I want to. Can I read him *Sleeping Beauty*?"

"Yes."

She begins to cry, and my heart breaks for her; only fifteen days ago, her whole world came crashing down, and now she's on the precipice of losing her "brother."

Ira, as it turns out, has not only lost his eyesight, he has also lost his continence, so once everyone is gone, I grab my computer, gather him up in a towel, and head to the bathroom so that the piss and shit can be contained to a smaller area.

Sitting on the black-and-white tile with Ira's head resting on my left knee, I prop my laptop up on the Bear's potty stool to use it for a desk. It's kind of the perfect place to write tasteless jokes that are frequently in opposition to my personal politics, and I'm only sorry it wasn't a venue that had ever occurred to me before now. It's July 24, but I'm writing for the month of September, which, from where I sit on the floor of the bathroom, seems so very far away:

> It's September 1st, and today in 1977, Fleetwood
> Mac is in the Top Ten with "Don't Stop."

I feel something warm and wet as I type, and realize that Ira is peeing. I push the potty stool and computer aside and mop up the piss with a hand towel, and as I do, I think about how hard it is, not to mention boring, to come up with jokes about the same groups over and over. I'd love to write about Janis, Joni, Linda, or Carole, but I'm not "allowed" to write about these classic female artists, as they are not considered "classic" *enough.* "The audience for this skews male," I am told whenever I suggest a story about a fabulous woman in the history of rock and roll. Oh, sure—I can write about Joan Baez, but only if it's *really* a story about Bob Dylan; I can write about Stevie Nicks, but only if it's a story about the fact that she fucked—or fucked over, or both—most of the members of Fleetwood Mac. I can certainly write about Yoko Ono, as long as it involves a lazy punch line about her controlling ways or her shitty singing. To bowdlerize the Beatles, I'd say I want a revolution, except that I need the job. Today, I have the added excuse that I have a script to deliver, and also my dog is dying.

I sit back down at the potty-stool desk and reposition Ira so that his head once again rests on my thigh, and I attempt to wrestle a punch line out of Rolling Stone Ron Wood leaving his wife of twenty-three years for a teenage cocktail waitress. *Jesus,* I think to myself, *she's a child.*

My mind drifts to thinking about my own child and what Ira's death will do to her. Knowing that this day was coming, Sam and I have consulted with shrinks and other "experts" who deal with children and bereavement. We've been told to include her in an "age-appropriate way" when we put Ira to sleep and to let her decide how much, if at all, she wants to be a part of his passing. To get our feet wet, I suppose, a few days after Sam and I announced our split to her, I went to the bookstore and picked up yet another sad dinosaur book by the same authors of *Dinosaurs Divorce*, this one called *When Dinosaurs Die.*

I didn't even get through the first page before the Bear began to cry.

"Dinosaurs have the worst, most terriblest lives ever!" she wailed. "No. More. Dinosaurs! I never wanna hear another dinosaur story again everrrrrr!"

So much for age-appropriate. *But honestly,* I think to myself, *I can hardly blame her. Dinosaurs did seem to have it rough. No wonder they became extinct.*

Back to Shaffer and jokes about Iron Maiden, ass play, "nooners," and Scott Baio.

Sometime midafternoon, Ira has another seizure. I try to make sure there is nothing in his way, nothing that can hurt him or fall on him, and though I feel like I have never seen anything worse in my life, I kneel right next to him, watching and waiting until it's over and I can hold and comfort him. When I do, I think about how, only four days before, I took him in for a transfusion. It was the only one we had left, and aside from being out of money, I knew that after this one, when he next felt crummy, I'd put him down, just as I had promised him that day in the examination room. Remarkably, after this transfusion, his red blood cell count nearly doubled, with his PCV going up to thirty-six. It had never been this high all year. No one—not Jim, nor any of the people who worked at Chelsea Animal Hospital—could believe it. And though I knew it couldn't last—that eventually we'd be here, if not covered in piss in the bathroom, waiting out seizures, here in the sense that we'd be preparing for the imminent end—with those miraculous numbers, I thought for sure he'd make it to his twelfth birthday, exactly one week away. Despite his amazing numbers, he seemed tired when I picked him up, and though he was walking on his own and wagging his tail gaily, I thought in truth he seemed only marginally better. He'd had a fever, they told me; I had to keep him on Benadryl overnight, as well as his usual meds. He didn't eat that night, but the next day seemed ravenous, inhaling boiled chicken and rice and several Whole Foods meatballs. For the next few days, he was terribly happy and like his old self, and then, out of nowhere, seemed out of sorts, disoriented, senile even, randomly peeing either next to the kitchen sink or in the Bear's room. *Could he have had a mild stroke?* I wondered.

With Ira once again stabilized, I continue working, stopping to mop up excrement, for the remainder of the afternoon. Shortly after five, I finish the script. I look at the clock and decide to change before Jim arrives. I am a mess, covered in piss and shit, and I also want to change into something soft, so that when Jim administers the fatal shot, Ira will pass lying against me wearing something that feels cozy. I close the laptop and move it and the potty stool to the side, arranging Ira carefully on his blanket.

"Be right back, sweetheart," I whisper, and I kiss his temple. "Just gonna change . . ."

I take off my soiled clothes and change into my James Perse sweatshirt-material skirt and a tank top. I catch a glimpse of myself in the full-length mirror on the closet, noticing the dark circles under my eyes and the strands of gray in my widow's peak, and I think I need to remember to make a color appointment. I step back into the bathroom. I see him. Not moving. Not blinking. Staring. Mouth pulled back in a grimace, teeth clamped down on his tongue.

Ira.

I had been gone for only two, maybe three, minutes.

Ira.

I kneel down and put my hands on his frail body.

Ira.

I lay my head on top of his body and cry. I stay there until Sam comes in with the Bear. They have come back to wait for Jim, who is still en route.

"He's gone," I say softly, turning to them standing at the door.

Sam kneels down and looks. He closes Ira's eyes.

"Ira died?" the Bear asks.

"Yes, sweetie," Sam says. "I'm sorry."

"But I was gonna read him a story."

"I know, sweetie, but he couldn't wait," Sam says, holding her as she begins to cry.

"Mama," she chokes out. "Try giving him 'True Love's Kiss'—so he can wake up and we can be here and he can hear the story and . . ."

Sam takes the Bear out of the bathroom and back up to Stella and Stella's two moms while I call Jim.

Our neighbors Todd and Bruce offer us the use of their car to transport Ira to the Fifth Avenue Emergency Hospital, since we can't get into Jim's office until the morning and we can't keep the body overnight.

I bundle Ira up in his blanket and towel, and Sam and I head to the parking garage. There is a young couple in the elevator who smiles at us when we step in.

"Aww," the man says. "Sleeping—so cute. Boy or girl?"

"Boy," I say. "And he's dead."

At the Fifth Avenue Emergency Hospital, we are ushered into an examination room, where a technician takes inventory. We are asked what our dog's name is; we say "Ira." The technician tells us he is so sorry for our loss and that *she* is a beautiful dog. *This has happened for nearly twelve years,* I think. There are apparently quite a lot of people who've never heard of Ira Gershwin or Ira Levin or Ira Glass, and because the name ends in an *a*, they assume Ira is a girl. It has always bugged the shit out of me. Never more so than right this minute.

"He," I tell the guy. "He's a boy."

"Oh, I'm so sorry," he says.

"It's OK," I say.

We continue to answer questions, sign things, etc.

"Will you be wanting to have her cremated?" he asks.

"Yes," I tell him. "But it's a *he*. Ira's a boy."

"Oh, yes, I'm so sorry. Him . . ."

More questions, more things to sign.

"Um, there is also the option of having her paw or nose print cast into white clay as a memento, or you can have them made into jewelry, like a silver pendant, or you can have her nose or paw print done in gold, though that's more expens—"

"He's a boy!" I yell.

Eventually, we are left alone with him to say our final goodbyes. Sam goes first, then me. I trace the freckle on his left thigh with my finger; I run my hand over his fur and gently pull his teacup curled tail; I kiss the ears that were big enough to hold all my secrets.

"I will think of you whenever I eat pizza crust," I tell him. "Or whenever I see a dead palm kernel lying in a Los Angeles street. Or whenever I walk past Sarah Jessica Parker's town house. Or whenever I see a ruby, because it's your birthstone. Or whenever I'm at the beach. I will not be able to listen to Dolly Parton for a long, long time, but when I do, I will think of you then, too."

The tech hands me Ira's collar and asks us if we want his blanket and the towel we had him wrapped in, but I say no. I cannot bear to take those things. I return to his side three times before I am finally able to get myself to leave.

We walk out onto the street. The air is moist and thick—one of those typical humid midsummer evenings—and though it feels like it will surely rain, it never does.

～

Eight days later, they call to let me know that Ira's ashes have arrived back at the hospital. I thank them and say I will get there as soon as I can. It takes me two whole guilt-ridden days before I can gather my nerves to go anywhere near that awful place. I feel I need to be sans Bear or anyone else, that this is an errand I need to do by myself.

My heart pounds as I approach the hospital, and I have an awfully difficult time getting myself to walk through the door. At the reception desk, after telling them my name and why I'm there, I wait, trying to not see any of the dogs who sit in the waiting area, or the ones wearing their bandages or their casts or their "cones of shame" being returned to their relieved owners.

"Remember," the technician doing the handoff says to an owner. "Don't let him lick!"

Once the receptionist comes back, I quickly scan the name tag to see that it's correct, then, tucking the package inside my bag, I push my way through the heavy glass doors and, with tears streaming, limp slowly down Fifth Avenue. I get only as far as Tenth Street, where I take an arbitrary right toward Sixth Avenue and find a stoop upon which to park myself for a long cry. I'm not sure exactly why I've ended up on Tenth, as opposed to any of the other lovely streets in the Village between Fifth and Sixth, but as I look around from my perch on the stoop, there is something about it that seems like the perfect spot. I had forgotten what a relatively quiet block Tenth is compared to the other more busily traversed streets, like Twelfth, where I used to live, or Ninth, where, with Sam, I had once hoped to. Aside from Washington Square Park, these streets are the place I gravitate to more than any other, where I feel the most "me."

I stay for a while, watching various workers in hard hats and masks renovate brownstones for families probably off to their summer pads to avoid the dust and noise and, of course, the city's blistering heat. I watch as they drill and saw and carry lumber, and I wonder how long their services will take and whether the contractors' promises about completion dates will be kept and how it will all look when the building and its sumptuous flower boxes are blanketed in snow.

Finally, I open the stapled-shut bag with the black-and-white print of the GI dog standing at Iwo Jima. Inside a flowered, Hallmark-looking tin box is a plastic baggie containing the remains of Ira. I can hold the whole thing in the palm of my hand. I remember driving home the day we got Ira at the mall in LA—Sam behind the wheel, me cradling our new puppy in the passenger seat and calling to tell Billy back in New York.

"I can almost hold him in the palm of my hand." I laughed. "That's how tiny he is!"

I think of the three of us later that first night—Sam, Ira, and me—huddled together in bed, not having the heart to leave the new puppy in his crate, because he was crying, yes, but mostly because he was so small. For a second, I think I must have imagined he was ever that small, that it was the corruption of nostalgia causing me to recall something that, until now, I had forgotten completely. But that long-ago day barrels through my doubt like the stubborn sun pierces through the slats of the demolished brownstone roof next to my stoop, and I know it's as real and true as I am sitting here. *I can almost hold him in the palm of my hand,* I had said, so happy, so delighted, having no clue that one day I'd say the same thing, only this time I'd be shattered.

"He's sand," the Bear will remark when I show her later. "Ira is now sand . . ."

And though this is true, it will be nearly impossible to fathom the fact that there, in a very ugly, cheapo container that looks like something that might house a Glade bathroom candle, is all that's left of my beautiful dog. How strange it is to think that something so large to me in terms of meaning, so full of life and import and most of all love, is, as the Bear will so aptly describe, sand. Sand that can slip through your fingers, blow away in the breeze, and be indistinguishable, save for the grayish hue, from any you'd squish between your toes as you stroll down the beach.

The beach.

I think of how much Ira loved it and how much I want to bring him back there, if only symbolically.

A few weeks later, I'm in East Hampton for a book event at the library. Before I head back to the city, I take a drive by myself to Atlantic Avenue Beach in Amagansett, where, walking along the shore, I release some of Ira's ashes. I watch them drift into the wind, absurdly trying to track the grains and traces to their final resting place, but once they're tossed, they seem to just evaporate—into the sand and the surf—until they are an indistinguishable part of the beach. Maybe this is the point—ashes to ashes, dust to dust—and though it hits me how beautiful it is that Ira is now forever a part of the mythical energy that is for me Amagansett, I am still glad that I reserve the rest of his ashes for myself. I have imagined that perhaps one day, should I ever own a home with a garden again, I will bury him there because, like the beach, he loved a good garden. But maybe not. Maybe I will want him with me in whatever dwelling I happen to inhabit for the rest of my days. There's a lot I can't know or predict in this present moment, and though I know it will be necessary to look back, this, too, will be for another day. For now, I can only move, as is the natural order of things, forward.

It will never cease to amaze me how nothing about knowing Ira was going to die for a year and twenty-one days prepared me for what it would be like when he was actually gone. In the days and weeks immediately following his passing, my heartache lifts only when the day ends and I can revel in the hope that he will visit me in my dreams. Ira, however, will not even make so much as a cameo.

And this will shock me.

In fact, I will be so stunned by Ira's absence from my dream life that the thought *Maybe he's pissed at me for selfishly keeping him alive* will play over and over in my mind, as if his appearance in *my* dreams is *his* choice.

For a long time, I will feel completely disconnected from him: I will not feel he's "living on in my heart" or "watching over me" or even "at peace" or in the supposed "better place" people always seem to speak of when offering platitudes to the bereaved. Mostly, I will believe him—or rather, his soul, or the entity that was once Ira—to be nowhere. There will be nothing whatsoever—no eerie moments or signs that make me sense his presence—until one day, about five months later. It will be December and suddenly cold, the sort of first-of-the-season chill that snaps us to attention. I will reach for the down coat I haven't worn in nine or so months and, pushing my hands into the pockets, I will feel them: Ira's poop bags. I will be unprepared for both the discovery and the simultaneous streams of tears that are seemingly lying in wait. It will not be long after this that I will dream of standing in a meadow of green grass and I will see him in the distance. I will call his name, and he will come running. He will get to me and begin jumping, dancing merrily, still like Snoopy, tongue out, tail wagging—the smiley-faced doggy of my dreams, finally, *finally*, in my dreams. Overjoyed, I will sink to my knees. "I've missed you, I've missed you, I've missed you," I will say as he inhales my face with his tongue. He will stop rather abruptly, emit a quasi-bark, and take off, beckoning me to follow, and I will for a while, until I see the cliff. I will know he is imploring me to follow him. "I can't," I will say, kneeling down to him. "I can't."

I will look at his face. His tongue will be out; his eyes will be shiny and bright. His mouth will be turned up in a smile. And I will think to myself in the dream, *Wow, he's happy—Ira is really, really happy.*

"I'm so sorry I was never able to let you go," I will tell him. "I wanted to be able to do that for you so very badly. But you left before I got to tell you. I love you. So, so much. And I will always love you."

And just as I say this, he will take off running toward the cliff. I will chase after him, calling his name, but will stop just before the edge. And just as it looks like he's about to go over, he will begin to somersault, then soar, higher and higher, until . . . he's gone. I will wake depressed and sad, interpreting the dream through the lens of all that I did wrong in my attempt to control the things that I simply could not—that is, until something tells me to share the dream with the Bear.

"It's OK, Mom," she will tell me. "You went as far as you could go. You went as far as you could, and then you realized you had to stop. I think Ira knew that all along. That's why he let you go . . ."

~

Sam won't pack up his stuff one day—rather, the stuff, like Sam, will seem to disappear slowly, over time. There will never be that moment when I have to watch him pack up his shit in one fell swoop, or even one when the deed is taken care of out of my presence and I have to return to find a whole side of the closet gone, save for some empty dry-cleaning plastic limply hanging on hangers. No. It will be more like

Sam's stuff simply evaporates into thin air, so that there are times when I have to strain to believe that the clothes, or even Sam, had ever been there to begin with.

As we enter this new territory over the months that follow, there will be many stops and starts, twists and turns, backs and forths, that play out. I will occasionally feel terrified that I have made a huge mistake, feel I am to blame, long to have Sam back, vow to myself that I can do it, that I can change myself into the perfect partner for him in every way. But just as soon as those feelings are stirred, whether it's in the same day or even the same hour, the voice within will talk me off the ledge and remind me of the fact that, at the very least, I can assume only 50 percent of the responsibility—for the demise, yes, but also, and perhaps more importantly, for whether or not there would have been any hope for reconciliation, or, as Stephen would put it, a "new marriage" between us.

People will always want to know whose decision it was—who left whom. For some reason, this will seem terribly important. For a while, as a sort of shorthand, I suppose, I will simply say that it was my decision—that I was the one who called it quits. It wasn't untrue. But it will always bother me that the sort of factual nitpickiness of being literal about who said or did what belies the fact that what really happened was the result of a great many precipitating events. And that the keyword is almost always *we*. To wit:

We stopped laughing, stopped communicating, gave up on being understood. Stress infected our days and nights, and resentments piled up. *We* took each other for granted. At our best, *we* had sunk into a friendship; at our worst, *we* had become estranged relatives who experienced each other only negatively. *We* fell out of love, each of us disconnecting from the other, withdrawing in our own ways, and making intimacy initially scarce, then impossible. *We* suffered and stewed, thinking that was more or less how everyone who was married felt. By the time *we* got to therapy, it had little to no effect, but *we* stayed married anyway, because the idea of divorce, and what it would do to us and to our families and our daughter, was so painful. *We* repeatedly said things like "we're trying," but the only thing *we* were *really* "trying" was to avoid the reality that our marriage had been over for years. And once *we* both got wise and finally, finally admitted to ourselves the terrible truth, *we* clung to each other, out of fear and desperation, hoping beyond hope that what was happening wasn't really happening.

It comes down to one of you having to be brave enough for both of you, Stephen had said, and I suppose that's true. But maybe a better way to look at it is that one of you has to find it within yourself to love your spouse again for just a minute more. Because, as weird as it sounds, it's an act of love to let someone go who's meant so much, so they can get on with the rest of their lives.

Of course, I won't understand this right away; it will take several years of sorting through the rubble of his "stuff" and my "stuff" in therapy, meditation, and just plain living, to arrive at a place wherein I am able to look back on my marriage to Sam and understand that, perhaps not symmetrically, perhaps not in equal measure, but ultimately, we both left each other. It will take me equally long to grasp that it's impossible to be defensive and empathic at the same time, but when I do, I feel so bad to have made someone I loved so much feel so fucking bad. And as easy and problematic as it is to go down the familiar rabbit hole of fault, it can be awfully bracing to accept that a part of yourself will always reside in someone else's truth.

It will not, however, be an easy road. It will get harder before it gets easier. Divorce sucks. It sucks if you are the one leaving; it sucks if you are the one being left. It is a death in which the corpse has to stay with you, in your home, rotting away, until you actually sign the papers that say "You're divorced!" And even then, it still sucks, because, as I mentioned, divorce seriously sucks.

But one day, it will suck less, and then it will suck even less than that. And then there will come a day when you are beyond the terribleness, beyond the pain, the sadness, the fights, the rage, the disappointment, the demise, the end of a dream that was maybe never really yours at all. And you will find yourself staring at a faded snapshot of you and your dog taken by the man who used to be your husband. The photo, at a dog birthday party in Laurel Canyon, is not the most glamorous of either of you, and while the image over time has grown dim, the ebullience in your expressions is unmistakable and still crystal clear, encapsulating perfectly not just the adoration you felt for your dog but also your unbridled devotion to the person on the other side of the lens. And even if you no longer recall the particulars of the day in the canyon, what you will remember, always, is how you were feeling, because it was the way you *always* felt then: happy. Ridiculously, couldn't-get-over-your-luck-that-you-were-newly-married-to-your-best-friend-and-madly-in-love-with-him-and-your-puppy-and-your-dreams *happy*. And what strikes you most as you scan the photo is not the fuzzy feelings, the broadness of your grins, the extravagant mirth—no. What stands out to you now, what is so startlingly obvious above all else, is your blissful ignorance: how, in this fleeting moment, you could have had *no possible clue* where life would take you, what it would all look like ten springs later, how very far away from that misty morning in the hills, high above Los Angeles, you would one day be. And all at once, you will realize that you spent the final, painful year in the life of your marriage and your dog trying desperately to go back to the day the picture depicts, only to learn, as the photographer Robert Frank once said, "You can capture life, but you can't control it."

~

You can never imagine the end at the beginning. You are so filled with love and light and hopes and dreams that it seems at that moment unfathomable. And just as you can't possibly conjure the image of breaking apart when you are knee-deep in the magical dewiness of your union's inception, when it's reached its climax, it's almost impossible to recall how filled with unadulterated bliss you felt at the dawn of everything.

But hopefully, "the end of all our exploring," as T. S. Eliot said, "will be to arrive where we started, and know the place for the first time." And when you arrive there, you will know how to choose, living in the face of calamity; you will know that the truth, whether obscured by shadow or in the brightest light, can often be very difficult to see, that even in times of tremendous loss, one can still find ways to celebrate that same loss's curious gifts. You will know that surrender does not necessarily stem from weakness, nor does it mean giving up. Rather, it means showing up fully and then letting go of how it was all supposed to look. You will know that you'd be nowhere without your sense of humor, because even on the very worst of days, the jokes still need to get written. And, though you will not want it to be true, you will know, finally, beyond a shadow of a doubt, that even if it doesn't always save the day—or the marriage, or the dog—love never dies.

And you will not only know the place for the first time, you will remember it forever.

ACKNOWLEDGMENTS

Deepest gratitude to the following people, who have been essential to the writing of this book:

My editor, Carmen Johnson, whose enthusiasm and support never wavered, no matter how many deadlines I missed.

My agent, Erin Hosier, for her savvy, her kindness, and her faith in me and this project.

Colin Dickerman, who knew what I was trying to get at before I understood it myself.

Leigh Flayton, whose counsel one night over dinner changed everything.

Michael Edelstein for his pep talks.

Eddie Burke for his rosary.

Florence Falk for listening to every word.

Mike Albo for reading, the endless conversations, and the best notes in the world.

Troy Surratt, Nathaniel Hawkins, David Munk, and Elisa Casas, who all know why.

And finally, Howard J. Morris, without whose love and boundless belief in me there would be no book.

ABOUT THE AUTHOR

Photo © 2017 Lorin Klaris

Nancy Balbirer is a writer and performer of stage and screen. She is the author of *Take Your Shirt Off and Cry: A Memoir of Near-Fame Experiences*. She lives in Los Angeles with her family.